What Others

"Dr. Craig makes emotional intelligence understandable. She shows why it's worth raising your EQ in a fun, easy-to-read book that illuminates the subject."

Cherie Carter-Scott, Ph.D.
#1 NYT bestselling author of *If Life is a Game, These are the Rules*

"Dr. Craig has captured the essence of emotional intelligence and translated it into an engaging, helpful set of exercises for people who are interested in developing their capacity as adults."

Judith Stevens-Long, Ph.D.
Author of *Adult Life: Developmental Processes*

"Jeanne Anne Craig's book is a Baedeker for the emotional traveler— don't leave home without it. This road map for the seeker of emotional intelligence provides us with the rationale for why we all need EQ and how to get it. Its simple, user-friendly format belies its wisdom and truth. It is by turns, funny, sage, pragmatic and touching. It is a 'must read' for everyone."

Pauline Lyttle
President, GenderCorp, Inc.

"Jeanne Anne's book takes Daniel Goleman's book on *Emotional Intelligence* to another level, making the concept of emotional intelligence accessible to everyone. I took her book on a trip and couldn't put it down. We all need to improve our EQ and this book gives us the tools."

Marvin L. Bittinger, Ph.D.
Professor of Mathematics Education Indiana & Purdue
Author of over 153 math textbooks

"Throw out your soft skills training programs and start using Dr. Craig's tonic for bad management and insufferable people at work. This book clearly and humorously helps people discover and implement the right stuff at work. I can't picture any business executive who won't improve their interpersonal effectiveness and leadership skills by using this book for themselves and their teams. Best of all, it provides and easy and fun way to learn."

Roger McAniff
Management Consultant, Author of *The Outrageous Manager*

"Lively and infinitely useful, Dr. Jeanne Anne Craig's book takes the mystery out of Emotional Intelligence and step-by-caring-step, offers clear, common-sense ways to bolster EQ and become happier and more fulfilled individuals in the process."

Eric L. Zoeckler
Syndicated columnist, *Taming the Workplace*

"When you need the wisdom of an elder, the warmth and acceptance of a mother and the light and guidance of a Higher Self, turn to this wonderful guide. Jeanne Anne's humorous stories and insights provide just the gentle and wise hand we need to guide our own journeys toward emotional intelligence."

Sophia Torelli
Reader's Advisory Librarian, King County Public Library, Seattle

"Jeanne Anne's book explains why some people are successful and some are not. It is a must read for educators, teachers and administrators. If you want to learn more about helping students become successful, read this book!"

Lynda Humphrey
Director Strategic Planning, Northshore School District (ret.)

"Clients come to *A Great Career* when they're ready to follow their dreams, or are—voluntarily or involuntarily—out of work. *It's Not How Smart You Are, It's How You Are Smart* and the life lessons Dr. Craig provides are an ongoing support system for those clients. Through humor and practical, step-by-step guidance on changing one's life through enhanced EQ, Dr. Craig establishes the foundation for professional success, as well."

Carole S. Barns
Principal, A Great Career, Inc.

It's Not How SMART You Are
It's HOW You Are SMART

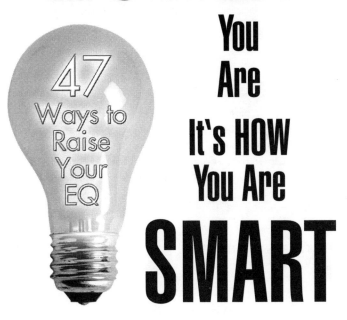

47 Ways to Raise Your EQ

Jeanne Anne Craig, Ph.D.

CRAINE PRESS
Kirkland, Washington

It's Not How SMART You Are It's HOW You Are SMART
47 Ways to Raise Your EQ

Jeanne Anne Craig, Ph.D.

Contact information:

Ꞇ Craine Press
218 Main Street, PMB #339B
Kirkland, WA 98033

Back cover photo: Kevin Gumke
Cover design and layout: Ad Graphics, Inc., Tulsa, OK
Printed in the United States of America

Publisher's Cataloging in Publication

Craig, Jeanne Anne.
    It's not how smart you are, it's how you are smart/
Jeanne Anne Craig. — 1st ed.
        p. cm.
    Includes bibliographical references and index.
    ISBN: 0-9710724-1-8

    1. Emotional intelligence.   I. Title.

BF576.C73 2002   152.4
                                   QBI01-201074

SONG OF THE OPEN ROAD, V

From this hour I ordain myself loos'd of limits and imaginary lines,
Going where I list, my own master total and absolute,
Listening to others, considering well what they say,
Pausing, searching, receiving, contemplating,
Gently, but with undeniable will, divesting myself of the holds that
    would hold me.
I inhale great draughts of space,
The east and the west are mine, and the north and the south are mine.

I am larger, better than I thought,
I did not know I held so much goodness.

All seems beautiful to me,
I can repeat over to men and women, you have done such good to
    me I would do the same to you.
I will recruit for myself and you as I go,
I will scatter myself among men and women as I go,
I will toss a new gladness and roughness among them.
Whoever denies me it shall not trouble me,
Whoever accepts me he or she shall be blessed and shall bless me.

                       – Walt Whitman
                       Leaves of Grass

for Terry

and

to the memory of my grandmother and muse
Mary Goldia Montgomery Jolliff

TABLE OF CONTENTS

ACKNOWLEDGMENTS

For services great and greater—there were no small services—I would like to thank the following :

Carole Barns, Sue Earnest, Ken Greff, Dale Hauer, Pat Morrison, and Ari Sasanoff for reading early drafts of the manuscript and for their critiques and comments.

Linda Davies for eagle-eyed line editing.

Bob Barta, the members of Speaking Professionally Toastmasters and the members of my Master Mind Group for encouragement and support.

Sue Earnest, Pat Morrison, Patty Spratley, Peggy Adams, Michael Lee Montgomery and Al Foxx for making me laugh.

Sharon Castlen for myriad services rendered.

Dottie Billington, Ph.D. for sharing the concept of 'pacers.'

My clients and workshop participants for sharing their stories.

Special thanks to my editor, Nancy Burkhalter, Ph.D.

Especially special thanks to my husband, Terry Swaine for everything.

INTRODUCTION

If you don't have it, it doesn't matter what else you have; if you have it, you don't need anything else.

— James M. Barrie

Mr. Barrie was speaking of charm, but he could have been speaking of emotional intelligence or EQ. When I was a school psychologist, I administered IQ tests, which did a good job of identifying smart people and predicting who would do well academically. Unfortunately, IQ tests are not so good at predicting who will be successful in life. It is emotional intelligence, EQ, or what I call the right smarts, that is the key to success, no matter how success is defined.

Bruce is technically brilliant. As project lead, it is an important part of his job to see that those in his group are up to speed on the software they need to get the project completed. Liz is the new hire who shares his cubicle at work. You'd think this would put her in a great position to learn what she needs to know, but the problem is, Bruce won't talk to her. He won't talk much to anybody. When she asks him a technical question he snarls that she should figure it out for herself. When she pointed out that she could be more efficient if only he'd answer some of her questions, he instructed her to communicate with him only by e-mail. This was better, but she still had questions she needed to ask and not wait for the answer. Finally after much persuasion, he decided to grant her an in-person audience everyday from 3:30 to 4:00 o'clock. Otherwise he told her to leave him alone.

Bruce certainly has a high IQ and is demonstrably capable in terms of technical ability, but his poor people skills are a problem to everyone around him. Most of us know a whiz kid who started out full of promise, but wound up flipping burgers or pumping gas; or we know of a hotshot high-level executive whose employees and coworkers view her with fear and loathing. The problem in all three cases is that these individuals have high intellectual abilities and well-developed technical skills, but they lack the key component to having a successful life. They're smart, to be sure, but they don't have the right smarts; they don't have emotional intelligence.

While we know there are interventions that raise IQ, such as good schooling, there are aspects of IQ that cannot be changed. Fortunately EQ is much more easily changed. Your emotional intelligence can be raised no matter what your age or circumstances. This book will give you a number of ways you can get the right smarts.

Throughout the book I will be using the three terms interchangeably: emotional intelligence, EQ, and the right smarts. In the first section, I discuss what EQ is through the eyes of some of the researchers. I then take a developmental view to raising emotional intelligence using heuristic devices. The second section of the book contains the heuristics, which are selected activities to try out or work through. Developmental psychologists have noted that there are various *developmental spurs,* which are grit in the oyster of emotional growth. Each of the heuristics is a developmental spur that has been shown to influence and create a climate in which emotional growth flourishes.

HOW TO USE
THIS BOOK

The book can be read in two ways: You may want to start at the beginning and read from cover to cover. Or you may wish to skip Part I altogether and read the chapters in Part II, either from start to finish, or at random. Either way, if you work on the suggestions in the book, you can't help but get the right smarts.

PART I

EQ
DEVELOPMENT

CHAPTER ONE

What Is Emotional Intelligence?

Change and growth take place when a person has risked himself and dares to become involved with experimenting with his own life.

— Herbert Otto

I 've been a school psychologist for more than twenty-five years. During that period I've administered over a thousand intelligence or IQ (Intellectual Quotient) tests. These tests are extremely useful for predicting school success. It's a no-brainer that if you're smart you probably do well in school and if you're not, school is going to be difficult for you. However, school success doesn't necessarily predict success in life. Paul was a classmate of mine who was well liked, but everyone knew he was no great brain. Once he wrote an essay that seemed beyond his abilities and our teacher asked him, "Paul, was this original?"

"Oh, no ma'am," Paul responded, "I wrote that myself." Paul got an award for perfect attendance at high school graduation. "I never missed a day in the whole fourteen years," he boasted in a joke that let us know he had repeated a grade. Poor school performance notwithstanding, Paul went on to own an extremely successful automobile agency, to be happily married to the same woman for more than 35 years before he died, and to raise three children who adored him. Paul had the right smarts, high emotional intelligence. Researchers are finding that the abilities that comprise emotional intelligence account for about two thirds of the success formula, however it is defined.

In the following section I explore new ways of defining intelligence and what makes up emotional intelligence.

New Ways of Looking at Intelligence

Howard Gardner, Harvard professor of education, believes our way of looking at intelligence has been too narrow. IQ tests have measured only a small set of abilities, typically verbal, logical-mathematical and spatial. In 1983, Gardner published his research on what he termed "multiple intelligences." His book, *Frames of Mind*, expanded our concept of intelligence to include four additional abilities not found among those measured on standard IQ tests. The first two concern musical and kinesthetic gifts. The remaining two, intrapersonal and interpersonal, are the skills that comprise emotional intelligence. Intrapersonal ability has to do with accessing your feelings. Interpersonal skills refer to your sensitivity to others.

Following close behind Gardner's research, Reuven Bar-On, a lecturer and psychologist at Tel Aviv University Medical, developed a formal psychological survey in 1985. This instrument attempts to measure what he calls "emotional quotient," thus the term EQ. In his view, EQ includes optimism, flexibility, and the ability to cope with stress and solve problems, as well as the ability to understand the way others feel and to maintain satisfying interpersonal relationships.

Peter Salovey, professor of psychology, epidemiology, and public health at Yale University, and John Mayer, psychologist at the

University of New Hampshire came to similar conclusions. In 1990. Salovey and Mayer published their study of "emotional intelligence." In their theory, emotional intelligence involves the ability to "monitor one's own and others' feelings and emotions, to discriminate among them and to use this information to guide one's thinking and actions."

Finally in 1995, with the publication of his bestseller, *Emotional Intelligence,* Daniel Goleman popularized the subject and brought it into public consciousness. Goleman expands his notion of emotional intelligence beyond the original concepts to include qualities of character such as compassion, self-discipline and altruism.

In this book, I propose to extend the theory, as well as provide a way to help you develop your own emotional intelligence.

CHAPTER TWO

The Developmental View of EQ

It doesn't happen all at once.
You become. It takes a long time.

– Margery Williams

As a developmental psychologist, my view of emotional intelligence is, naturally enough, developmental. My grandmother would've called it maturity, or being on-target in the growing up process. A baby starts out as a completely egocentric being. He is the only one in the relationship with needs and is not aware of your needs. He may, in fact, fulfill your need to be a nurturing caretaker, but this is not through any effort on his part. Fortunately babies are adorable and we don't mind that they are demanding and egocentric. However, this same behavior in a 35-year-old is distinctly less than charming. Dealing with the developmental tasks we encounter as we progress through the lifespan allows us opportunities to raise our emotional intelligence.

Developing EQ is a hero's journey. The late Joseph Campbell, author of *The Hero With a Thousand Faces,* described it as a quest we set out on during which we leave our comfort zone and venture into unknown territory. Inevitably we encounter dragons—forces with which we grapple, and in the struggle we emerge with the grail. The struggle is painful, perhaps, but definitely worth the journey.

The Central Developmental Task

We all face the struggle between two opposing forces: the drive to develop a self and the opposite drive to be part of the group. When I am developing self, I am discovering what *I* want, who *I* am, doing what *I* want to do. I'm developing my talents and interests and following my whims and desires. When the force is in the other direction, I want to be included as part of a couple or group, so I find it necessary to consider what *you* want, to negotiate, to cooperate, to compromise, to conciliate.

A confirmed bachelor, absorbed in developing himself and his career, turns in the opposite direction to marry and create a life with a partner. An empty-nest mother, having spent a large portion of her life on the development of others, changes directions, venturing out into her own career. Throughout the life span, the pendulum is swinging back and forth—self-to-other-to-self-to-other. The balance is tricky and hard to achieve, but in the process of attempting the balance, we develop emotional intelligence. Our rough edges are smoothed off, our facets begin to glitter and glow. We become.

Brain Development

Cogito ergo sum. (I think, therefore I am).

– Descartes

Reptiles and badly frightened people have two things in common: They have no sense of humor and they eat their young.

– David Schnarch

23

To widen the developmental lens in our view of emotional intelligence, it is helpful to understand how the brain evolved. The brain stem, also referred to as the reptilian brain, is the part that controls basic functions. It was the earliest part to develop, and is responsible for survival activities such as breathing and digestion. Later in our evolution came the limbic system or mammalian brain. This is the part that controls emotion. We share with other mammals, for example, a concern for our young. Turtles and snakes lay their eggs and leave their young to fend for themselves. In fact, young snakes have to move pretty fast if they are to survive.

The last part of the brain to develop is the neocortex, or thinking brain. This is the part that allows us to reason and make logical choices. Since the neocortex is the last to develop, it stands to reason it is the most highly evolved, hence, somehow better and more valuable than parts that developed earlier. It is no secret that our culture places a higher value on the thinking, reasoning functions than on those devoted to feelings and emotions. However, to do so is to make a mistake, according to Antonio Damasio, author of *Descartes' Error*.

When Damasio worked with people who had the parts of their brain destroyed that controlled emotion, he found they could reason and think clearly and logically, but could not make decisions or function beyond a fairly primitive level. Damasio concluded that when the thinking brain is divorced from the emotional brain, it is no more able to perform than a brain that is running purely on emotion. It is the interworking of feelings and logic, the combination of which is the *human brain*, that is what we are using when we are behaving in emotionally intelligent ways.

The mammalian brain operates many times faster than the thinking brain. This works out pretty well for us if we're in danger. Let's say, for example, we're camping, and we wake up and hear something crashing around in the bushes. The mammalian brain has us jumping up and at the ready for bears long before our thinking brain figures out our camping partner made a midnight potty call. But sometimes the speed at which the mammalian brain works gets us in trouble. If it had been an actual bear, this fast action might prompt us to shoot the dangerous beast. But what if we shot first, only to discover it was the partner with the full bladder causing the commotion? Some version of this scenario is at work in episodes of road rage. The Ready, Fire, Aim Syndrome. This is operating out of pure emotion without the intervention of the thinking brain.

As we can see, attempting to operate solely with either the emotional or the thinking parts of our brain has us functioning at a pretty low level of emotional intelligence. The person with the right smarts, the high EQ individual is able to pause long enough before acting to use the integrated human brain and make the truly smart decision.

This has been a deliberate oversimplification of brain development. For those who wish to understand this process in more detail, refer to more scientific explications in the reference section, particularly books by Antonio Damasio and Joseph LeDoux.

The Emotionally Intelligent Individual

Building character is like making bread—you have to mix it little by little, step-by-step and moderate temperature is needed.

– Roshi Sunryki Suzuki

A person with high emotional intelligence has learned to integrate the parts of her brain and uses the 'human brain' in most circumstances. She has a solid sense of herself that is non-negotiable in any context. Such a person is able to stay within integrity and to operate out of her values. Achieving it is a growth process that psychologists have called by several different names. Psycho-analyst Carl Jung called it individuation; family therapist, Murray Bowen called it differentiation.

A person with high emotional intelligence has the ability to stay calm and centered and to maintain a sense of self in the presence of others, especially those with whom she has an emotional connection. People who have developed a high level of emotional intelligence can maintain their course when important people in their lives are upset with them or pressure them to agree and conform. They can, in fact, agree without feeling they've given themselves up and can disagree without being paralyzed with anxiety over losing a relationship. It's like the old joke that says maturation (high EQ) is the ability to do what you want to do even if your parents approve of your choice. When we have high EQ we can stay connected with people even when we disagree with them.

High EQ people can assimilate a high level of stress and have the ability to be around anxious people without absorbing and passing on the anxiety. In addition, high EQ people have qualities of compassion, altruism, self-discipline, optimism, flexibility and the ability to solve problems and cope with stress. They are able to read and monitor their own feelings and those of other people. They can maintain satisfying interpersonal relationships. Finally, and to me one of the most important qualities of all, they have a sense of humor and are fun to be around.

Have I just described a saint? I hope not. I have confidence that an ordinary mortal can be this sort of person. We'd like to spend our time hanging out with people like this and, please, Lord, we'd like to *be* people with qualities like these. With the right kind of effort on our part, we can develop these qualities.

CHAPTER THREE

Involuntary EQ Development

Perhaps when a soul has been tampered with, deformed, there is always the possibility that it will return to its shape once again, a gold cell filled with a sweetness we call love.

– Dorianne Laux

D evelopment proceeds along several paths. We have developmental tasks to master and are faced with developmental crises to deal with. These are mandatory. We are not given choices about whether or not to deal with these issues.

Developmental Tasks

Developmental tasks are those activities we all go through, such as learning to walk and talk, going to school, and making decisions regarding careers and life mates. As we go through each of these challenges, we grow, develop and change. Once we have gone through one of these processes, we see the world in a new way and we can never go back and be the person we were before. The second kind of spur to our development involves various kinds of crises.

Developmental Crises

Life presents us with other growth experiences, most of which we would never choose on our own. Some of these we go through along with everyone else in our age group. These include major disasters, such as earthquakes, floods, droughts, wars and economic depressions. These shared experiences shape our development. For example, the generation that grew up during the depression tend, as a group, to be thrifty, to abhor waste and to value giving a full day's work for a day's pay.

Other unpredictable crises include house fires, disastrous accidents and illnesses, and the untimely loss of loved ones. Faced with the choice of going through any of these ordeals, most of us would say, "Let this cup pass from me." However, we have only to pick up a copy of the *Reader's Digest* or one of the *Chicken Soup* series to read the personal accounts of individuals who have undergone trials such as these and who feel that going through these experiences was the making of them as a person. Professional speaker and comedian Al Foxx was an exuberant 19-year-old when he had the motorcycle accident that left him a hemiplegic. He was told he'd never walk or talk again, let alone drive. He has defied the odds by doing all three. He has "a little hitch in his gitalong," as the late Tennessee Ernie Ford would have said, but he's walking. He not only talks, he is an inspirational and motivational speaker with a powerful message about triumphing over adversity. And his brochure says, "Look out, he's driving!" *The Seattle Times* calls him "The world's funniest brain damaged comedian." Al would never have willingly chosen the ordeal he suffered, but he has turned the tragedy into a positive model for us all.

All of the experiences I've listed above are what developmental psychologists refer to as *developmental spurs*. They are the sand in the oyster of our lives that nudge us ever higher on the developmental scale. As I have said, they are transformational in nature. We go in as a certain kind of person and emerge on the other side different. We are irrevocably changed, for we will never again view the world in quite the same way after going through these experiences. These are 'make or break' experiences; not everybody who goes through them changes in positive ways.

> *We all start off with the same capacities, but some people develop them and others don't.*
>
> – Dalai Lama

CHAPTER FOUR

Voluntary EQ Development

We humans are given a significant role in determining ourselves through the ways we choose to grow.

– Robert Cooper

While we have no control over the involuntary developmental spurs, this book is about the voluntary ones—the ones we can choose to undergo. If we all had our 'druthers, these are the ones we would choose, if, in fact we chose any at all. In the process of choosing and working through these, we're more likely to experience slight discomfort, rather than the outright pain we may sometimes feel dealing with the involuntary spurs. And sometimes what we feel isn't discomfort at all, but elation or the contentment that comes from being in flow.

What I am proposing is that rather than bowing to the inevitable, we attempt to impose some guidance on the process. We try to get it to turn out more the way we want it to.

Why Bother to Develop EQ?

Pain is about the resistance to the motion of life.

— Robert Kegan

Man is a pleasure-seeking, pain-avoiding animal, but we are such a contrary species that we seem more highly motivated to avoid pain than to seek pleasure. It is true that those with high EQ are more successful in life, but some people, it seems, are not motivated to seek success. Avoiding the downside of *not* developing EQ may be more motivating for these folks than the positive pursuit of success.

So what does it cost not to develop EQ? Where is the pain associated with avoiding growth? It is this: When we are reluctant to move out of our comfort zone into the seemingly treacherous waters of self-development, life becomes monotonous and we gradually become bored. Eventually life lacks color and meaning and problems grow and fester. If we don't push through this pain and endure the anxiety of growth, we ultimately feel a deadness that makes us at risk for substance abuse or suicide. Or we decide to try and remake ourselves by dumping our current mate in favor of a new life with (or without) someone else. Perhaps we try adrenaline-pumping activities in the hope they will make us feel more alive. Unfortunately, many, if not most of us have a higher tolerance for the pain of not growing than we do for the anxiety that crops up when we try to change. But the cost of not doing so is high.

Become who you are.

— Neitzsche

The Heuristic Approach

We have the picture in our heads—the ideal life. The lovely home filled with beautiful objects, the perfect mate with whom to share it, trips to exotic places where we bare our perfect bodies to the sun. We can see it vividly; we can smell the ocean, feel the sand between our toes, hear the gulls cry. We see it and we want it. Now!

Why not? It's the American way. We want what we want when we want it. And we will pay any amount to discover the *25 Steps to Instant Success,* how to *Get Rid of Jiggly Arms in Only 10 Minutes a Day,* or *50 Ways to Lose your Lover!* We're looking for algorithims. An algorithm is a precise set of steps that leads to a desired outcome. When we follow the steps in the prescribed order, we can tick off the tasks as we accomplish each one, knowing we're that much closer to achieving our desire—washboard abs or a blue-chip portfolio.

It would be nice if life worked that way, but people don't operate by algorithms. Machines do, computers do, and probably robots do, but human growth and development follows a much less clear path. When we are after something as ephemeral as a successful life, the very best we can do is to follow heuristics.

What Is a Heuristic?

It's pronounced hyoo-ris'-tik. Think of a heuristic as a lens to look through, an experience to try out, an exercise to go through, a way of thinking to try on. According to Michael Ray and Rochelle Myers, authors of *Creativity in Business,* "a heuristic is an incomplete guideline or rule of thumb that can lead to learning or discovery." It comes from the same Greek root as the word eureka, what Archimedes was said to have shouted as he ran nude through the streets after he grasped the concept of displacement while in his bathtub.

By engaging in a heuristic, by trying on the lenses, by looking through them for a period of time, one makes serendipitous discoveries. We don't always know the outcome, but if we stay with the experience we may discover something interesting, exciting or wonderful. Of course, you may wish to temper your enthusiasm and not run nude through the streets, although you certainly could learn something interesting that way!

In the process we will change; we will be transformed. We will raise our EQ. Developing EQ is similar to building our muscles. We work to stress the muscle fibers. The right amount of stress produces growth. No stress, no growth. No pain (or at least the discomfort of change) no gain.

There is no single, one-size-fits-all route to the development of EQ. Everyone's path is different. The heuristics in this book will have varying degrees of value to each person at different times in their lives. Each of the following chapters in the book is a heuristic designed to stretch us, to help us to see the world in a new way, to try something new, or to nudge us out of our comfort zone. Some may be of no use to you at all while others may be just what you need to do for yourself at this particular time in your life. And at another period, the ones that seemed worthless the first time through may be what you need at this different phase you are in.

If you are forced to do your personal homework,
you end up knowing who you are.

– Jennifer James

"Change Back!"

All growth is costly. It involves leaving behind
old ways of being in the world.

– Robert Kegan

Don't expect the growth path to be entirely smooth. Change is difficult and there may be some negative reactions. People accustomed to the old you may become anxious and say to you either directly or indirectly, "Change back, change back." These may even be some of the same folks who have been telling you for years they want you to change.

Expect negative reactions in yourself, as well. You're not used to you this way either, so your system may also tell you to change back. It does this by throwing the system into temporary chaos. You may lose things, feel a little off, or become slightly confused. If you recognize this as part of the process and not a true obstacle, you can stay the course. The payoff is high and the cost of not doing so is ultimately feeling half-dead.

Oh, grow up!

– Joan Rivers

Characteristics of Emotional Intelligence

Those whose intellectual functioning can retain relative autonomy in periods of stress are more flexible, more adaptable and more independent of the emotionality about them. They cope better with life stresses, their life courses are more orderly and successful and they are remarkably free of human problems.

– Murray Bowen

High Emotional Intelligence	• Believes in the rights and dignity of all people. • Doesn't impose values on others but feels all should respect others' rights. • Has a solid sense of self and can function autonomously during times of increased anxiety. • Is self-motivated and can delay gratification. • Has satisfying personal relationships. • Copes successfully with broad range of human situations.
Moderately High Emotional Intelligence	• Is responsible, "good" citizen. • Acts to maintain self-respect. • Has developed a reasonable sense of self, but can be susceptible to the emotion and anxiety in a situation. • Moderately high levels of motivation, delaying gratification. • Fairly satisfying personal relationships. • Copes with most human situations.
Moderately Low Emotional Intelligence	• Is defined a great deal by what others think and tends to direct life energy toward this rather than personal goals. • Is more forgiving and flexible than lower levels. • When anxiety is low, can function well, but regresses when anxiety is higher. • Self-esteem dependent on others. • Lacks a solid sense of self. • Fairly low levels of satisfaction with relationships.
Low Emotional Intelligence	• Has a "what's in it for me" attitude. • Poorly developed sense of self. • Has poorly defined goals and no plan for achieving them. • Is in dependent relationships, borrows strength to function. • Poor ability to sustain relationships. • Expends much energy keeping anxiety at bay. • Chaotic lifestyle. • Does not take responsibility for actions, finds blame outside self.

PART II

HEURISTICS

GETTING DOWN TO BASICS

People with highly developed emotional intelligence share certain fundamental characteristics and abilities. The heuristics in this section of the book focus on those traits and on ways to grow them in ourselves.

Learn Your Non-Negotiables

It is important to let people know what you stand for. It's equally important that they know what you won't stand for.

– B. Bader

What are your non-negotiables? This is a question I ask my audiences as well as my therapy and coaching clients. What are your bottom-line items? What would cause you to go to the wall, to leave a relationship or job, to go to battle? These are your non-negotiables. I have learned, for example, that I am not willing to stay in a relationship with someone who lies to me. If I'm lied to by someone who sells me something, it's simple; I don't shop there anymore. If we're going to be interacting with each other over time, tell me the truth or I'm outta here. It's non-negotiable with me.

Jane married a man who changed jobs and moved frequently. When a work situation in one town didn't pan out, he bought a plane ticket and was off to greener pastures. Early in the marriage, this was exciting. But after they had children, it lost some of its luster. By the time their three daughters were in school, this lifestyle became more and more difficult for her to sustain. Jane gradually came to realize that having a home she could count on living in and not changing the children's school were non-negotiable items for her. Finally when one more job went upside down and her husband insisted they move to another state, she took a stand. She insisted they stay put and that he find another job locally. When he refused, she ended the marriage, although it was the most frightening thing she had ever done in her life. A non-negotiable had been violated for too long.

It takes a while to know what our non-negotiables are. Usually we learn by having them ignored over time. Living too long with violations of our non-negotiables compromises our integrity. We feel as if we've sold out if we put up with it. Eventually this becomes such an energy drain that we must change the situation or feel half-dead. Learning what your non-negotiables are is a building block for establishing appropriate boundaries. Once you know your non-negotiables, you can set limits on the behavior of others without feeling guilty.

I tell couples it is of the utmost importance that they get in touch with their bottom line items. If you can live with another person's non-negotiables, the relationship has a chance. If not, it's doomed. Daniel wants to have children; his wife Pamela does not. They are at an impasse. Both feel this is a non-negotiable for them. If one of them does not change his or her mind, their marriage will probably come to an end, or one of them will have to live with a major resentment for the rest of his or her life.

Sometimes we encounter our non-negotiables at work. Nikki has a boss who is verbally abusive. He likes to say of himself that his bark is worse than his bite, but the insults he yells when he is angry have hurt and humiliated Nikki far longer than she is comfortable with. She is now at the stage where she realizes she can no longer tolerate such behavior. She's face to face with a non-negotiable and her boss must either change his behavior or Nikki will take a stand and change jobs.

In my workshops, I tell people there is an optimal number of non-negotiables, but I don't know what it is. I do know that if you have too many, you're a terminal grouch and a very difficult person to be around. If you don't have enough, you're an impossible weenie and people are going to run all over you.

I remember one workshop participant who said that having her children make their beds everyday was a non-negotiable. I cautioned her to think very carefully about this. Having strong feelings about something is not the same as being willing to leave the scene if the terms aren't observed. Is she going to divorce her kids if they don't make their beds? To give them up for adoption?

Non-negotiables are not trivial. In fact, if someone would leave a relationship because of an unmade bed, it wouldn't be the bed that was at issue, but some underlying cause such as a feeling that one's desires were too often ignored by the other party. Learning our non-negotiables is an important building block to developing the right smarts.

In matters of principle, stand like a rock.

— Thomas Jefferson

HEURISTIC

Begin to be familiar with your non-negotiables. Observe carefully when you feel hurt, angry or insulted. Is this a non-negotiable for you? Are you truly willing to take serious action over this, no matter what the cost?

Set Appropriate Boundaries

When you love someone, you do all you can for them, without giving yourself away.

– Virginia Satir

In the shifting balance between developing self and developing relationships, most of us have a tendency to over-develop one side, and as a consequence, the other side is left wanting. Those whose primary emphasis is on the relationship side often have a hard time setting limits on the behavior of others; they don't have clearly established boundaries.

Cassie has trouble establishing appropriate boundaries. Cassie is a pleaser who likes to be helpful and who cares a great deal what other people think of her. Too much! Because of this, people tend to take advantage of her. Her family takes her for granted. Not only do her husband and two teenage children not appreciate what she does for them, they don't even notice. What's to notice? She runs a demanding consulting business in addition to doing all the family cooking, shopping, laundry and most of the cleaning. She adds to this a chauffeur service for the kids, who don't have cars yet. No one says thanks. Do you thank the moon for coming out at night?

Clients also violate her boundaries. Cassie allows her customers to abuse her by not paying on time, or sometimes not at all, and by being late for appointments or staying beyond their allotted time without payment. All this would be okay if it made Cassie happy or if she were a candidate for sainthood who lived to serve. But the fact is, she is unhappy and resentful.

Some people are exquisitely sensitive to others' boundaries, even those that are not explicitly stated. It's as though there is a force field around each person and these perceptive souls grasp this instinctively and don't violate boundaries. If everyone were like this we wouldn't need to establish clear boundaries. Alas, most of us need things to be more specific.

The amazing thing is, while you'd think it would be good to be around people with poor boundaries, it's actually no fun. You'd think you'd be able to have your way more often with individuals like this, or not have to negotiate so fiercely. Well, that part's true, but the downside of being around these folks is, you often injure their feelings without being aware of it, and then you feel like a jerk.

You may find out about this through a third party, as people with poor boundaries tend to be conflict phobic, as well. And rather than confront the violator, they are likely to bring in someone else to tell about it. If I'm the violator, this makes me feel like a big, insensitive mule when I find out about it. I also feel a little injured myself since I seldom knowingly do anything hurtful, and if I do so without meaning to, I feel mortified by my klunky behavior. And I feel resentful that a third party was brought in to judge my behavior, and not a little paranoid that my friends are talking about me behind my back.

Everyone wins when boundaries are clear. If I set clear boundaries, I'm protected from the damaging behavior of others. If you set them, I don't have to tiptoe around you in order not to offend you. Get clear on what is and is not acceptable behavior from other people toward you. When there is a violation, calmly and even lovingly let the other person know, and request the change in behavior that's called for. If you've always had trouble establishing boundaries, you need to raise your own awareness level to detect these violations early on, when they are minor annoyances, rather than major violations. Sometimes that feels petty, but until your boundaries are no longer being violated, this is the heuristic for you.

HEURISTIC

Learn to establish appropriate boundaries. Everyone wins when people make their boundaries clear to those around them.

Be Assertive

> *Selfishness is when someone places his*
> *own comfort before your convenience.*
> — Joan Tepperman

ssertiveness training had its heyday in the mid-seventies. Then, somehow it fell out of favor. I never see it listed in the extended education section of our local community college these days. Possibly it's considered old hat. Nevertheless, high EQ people are appropriately assertive.

But aren't assertive people obnoxious and over-bearing? Absolutely not. If the behavior is obnoxious, it's aggression, not assertiveness. We are assertive when we calmly defend our boundaries. Author Anne Lamott says we are each allotted an emotional acre, an amount of psychic space we are all entitled to. If I intrude onto your acre, I'm aggressive; if I allow you to intrude on mine, I'm passive. If I passively allow you to violate my boundaries and then quietly get even, I'm being passive aggressive. When we are assertive we are being direct and honest with people and we are not pretending to feel a particular way in order to meet with their approval.

Jarris mostly keeps his distance with people and, predictably enough, he feels lonely. He is uncomfortable being around people because he is unable to let them know in a clear way when they have invaded occupied territory. Rather than run into a situation that makes him uncomfortable he avoids contact. Jarris has an inadequate sense of entitlement. After his parents' divorce, it fell to Jarris to take care of his devastated mother. In her pain, she demanded his time, energy and attention to a degree that was a violation of his boundaries. Being a kind and gentle soul, he felt sorry for his mother and was afraid she was too fragile to handle direct messages that she was doing so. He never learned to stand up for himself so now he stays away from people to avoid having to.

Being assertive means learning to say the "N" word: No! I have yet to encounter anyone who actually likes saying no to people, but it is necessary from time-to-time if we are to maintain our boundaries. If someone makes a request that isn't right for you in some way, one of you is going to feel a certain degree of discomfort, no matter what your answer is. If you say no, the other person suffers; if you say yes, it's going to be you. You get to choose.

Vanessa is another gentle soul who can't bear to say no to her kids. She can't stand to see the look of disappointment in their eyes, or hear their cries of anguish when they don't get what they want. But in saying yes inappropriately she often causes distress and worry not only to herself but to her husband, who usually has to be the bad guy and say no to the kids to keep them safe and himself free of undue anxiety. Your lack of assertiveness certainly causes you problems, but often becomes problematic for those around you, as well.

If you have trouble with assertiveness, examine your feelings of entitlement. On some level, do you feel undeserving? Do you not feel entitled to your emotional acre; to take up your share of the available psychic space? What unresolved issues from your past have set such a pattern in place? What can you do to establish a new pattern?

If you find it hard to say no, learn to learn to pause and say, "Let me think about that and get back to you," when a request comes in. That way you avoid a knee jerk 'yes' response and you have a little space to consider whether you really want to respond affirmatively.

If you would like some further information about how to become more assertive, read, *How to Say No Without Feeling Guilty*, by Breitman, Hatch and Carlson.

> *If we do not take care of ourselves first,*
> *we become useless in helping others.*
>
> — **Anonymous**

HEURISTIC

Learn to be assertive. Get comfortable with your own emotional acre and defend your territory. Learn to pause before you automatically say yes.

Be "Integrous"

Think nothing profitable to you which compels you to break a promise, to lose your self-respect, to hate any person, to suspect, to curse, to act the hypocrite, to desire anything that needs walls and curtains about it.

– Marcus Aurelius

I've looked it up. *Integrous* isn't a word; it isn't in the dictionary. "Well, if it isn't a word, it should be," my grandmother would write in her letters to me when she coined a clever and appropriate term. Integrous is the word my friend Marge uses to mean being in integrity, which *is* in my dictionary. The definition is: "The state of being whole, entire or undiminished." Being integrous is living in accordance with your set of values and moral principles. It is walking your talk. People with high EQ strive to live their lives in integrity.

"The discrepancy between what we say we believe and what we actually do is a barometer of the degree of internal conflict in our lives," says management consultant Rhoberta Shaler. Most of us have an indicator that tells us when we are not being in integrity. Something nags at us; we feel just a touch sick to our stomachs, a bubble off plumb. We have a core set of values that determine

50

who we are. They are there, whether we have articulated them or not. When we do something, large or small, that violates these values, we get that little tug that tells us we've sprung an energy leak—so tiny we can't hear its hiss, but deflating us just the same.

There are people who do not have this internal, emotional gyroscope. Those identified as sociopaths and psychopaths operate without this guidance, to their cost and our peril. Sociopaths can "beat" a lie detector because they do not have the galvanic skin response or spike in blood pressure or heart rate that register for the rest of us when we lie. A great many of these folks populate our jails and prisons. Ultimately, the cost of living without integrity is high.

Sometimes we don't behave integrously because we're not sure what it is we believe in. Research demonstrates that people are healthier, physically, emotionally, and spiritually when they have a clear belief system and then behave in accordance with it.

Living an integrous life is not always easy. Think of the grief that a "whistle-blower" goes through. The movie, *The Insider,* portrays a man who lost his job, home, family, and friends when he revealed inside facts about the tobacco industry that had been misrepresented to the public. Being true to our value system can be costly, especially when we encounter a situation with two conflicting values, such as the ones faced by the protagonist in the movie. Do I do the right thing by informing the public, but in the process, betraying my friends and coworkers; or do I do the right thing in allowing my family to continue in the life I've provided for them, but remaining quiet and living with my troubled conscience? Which one is the right thing to do? Being in integrity sometimes means having to make hard choices.

My family had little money when I was growing up. When I was about nine, a family friend was visiting and went to the store with my father and me. We made our purchases and paid at the checkout counter. The clerk gave my dad too much change and when he discovered it, he brought it to her attention, giving her back the amount she'd overpaid. When we got outside, the friend expressed amazement and not a little scorn at that turn of events. I can still hear my dad saying, "Well, at least I can sleep at night with a clear conscience." My dad set a wonderful example of living integrously.

HEURISTIC

My grandmother gave me a diary for my tenth birthday. On the flyleaf she inscribed, "Never do anything you would be ashamed to write in these pages." That is the heuristic.

Take Authentic Action

> *Every human being is treacherous to every other human being because he has to be true to his own soul.*
>
> – D.H. Lawrence

What does it mean to take authentic action? This is a term Maria Nemeth uses in her book *The Energy of Money* to mean cutting through excuses, seeing things for what they really are, taking responsibility for yourself and taking positive steps toward solving a problem or coming closer to your life goals.

Zach wants to write a novel, but too many circumstances prevent him from doing it. He is too tired at the end of the day to be creative and not being a morning person, getting up and writing before work is out of the question. Then there is the problem of needing to exercise to stay in shape. By the weekend he needs to recharge his batteries so he spends time on the golf course or kayaking. In the winter there is skiing. There is no time to write a novel. For Zach, taking authentic action would mean making a true commitment to write, finding a time during the day and on weekends to write and then doing it. He could continue to find reasons for not doing it and at the end of his life he could get the equivalent of an excused absence, but for what? If he wants to be an author, he needs to take authentic action.

Alison is worried about her financial future. She is married to a forceful, high-energy go-getter, and being of a fairly passive nature, it is easier for her to let Cole have his way than to stand up to him. Cole fancies himself a high roller who feels no need of a plan for retirement, as he believes he will be able to fund their retirement from the millions he will make when his next deal comes to fruition. Cole and Alison are in their 40's and no nearer to the millions than when they married fifteen years ago. If Alison wants to have a financially secure old age, she must take responsibility for herself and take a stand for what she needs and then take authentic action toward achieving it.

Taking authentic action is really scary because usually there is a cost to doing it that we'd rather not pay. Complaining or dreaming about change is easier. The only cost is that you stay in a situation that's making you unhappy. We're often more willing to tolerate the pain of staying the same, than to deal with the anxiety of changing a situation. Or we dull the pain with our drug of choice, but we know that the situation stays the same.

Do something scary—or face
the problems from not doing it.
– David Schnarch

HEURISTIC

Discover what's holding you back from achieving your goals. Take stock of what the cost would be and the necessary activity to achieve the goals, and then take authentic action.

Learn to Soothe Yourself

---

*Anger is the feeling that makes your
mouth work faster than your mind.*
— Evan Esar

This may well be the most important tool you can use to raise your emotional intelligence. Much of our personal and relationship distress comes out of inadequately processed and managed anxiety. Any tool that will aid in the management of anxiety will automatically enhance a relationship and is an absolute necessity for raising EQ. When I was a school psychologist, one of my jobs was to work with troubled kids. I used to run "friendship groups" for small groups of kids who were having social difficulties. In plain English, that means I was trying to rehabilitate Public Enemies One through Six in the third grade.

These guys (yes, they were almost always guys) were usually holy terrors on the playground. Something that stood out about them was that they had so few choices about how to behave under stress. If they got accidentally bumped on the playground, they believed they had no recourse but to bop somebody back immediately, which almost always got them in trouble. They were genuinely perplexed, because it was clear to them that if someone bumped into you he needed to be taught a lesson. They truly felt it was unfair that they got punished for retaliating with their fists.

All the lectures in the world weren't getting through to these mini-thugs. Finally I hit on something that did get through. I drew the illustration below.

Basically what I said to them was that these pictures represent a Calm Guy and a Mad Guy. When you're calm, blood can get into your brain so your brain is full and you are smart. When you're mad, the blood leaves your brain and goes to your hands and feet and to your tongue, so your brain is empty and you're stupid. Where the blood is, the action is. You can think clearly and do smart stuff if your brain is full, but if the blood is all out in your hands and feet and tongue you do stupid stuff, like hit or kick people or you say things you shouldn't. So, if you can find a way to stay calm, you stay smart and smart people stay out of trouble.

Make sense? It made sense to the Purple Gang I was dealing with. We worked on ways to keep blood in their brains and their outlaw activities on the playground began to decrease.

Okay, this isn't completely scientifically accurate, but it's not too far off the mark. The fact is when we become overwrought under stress, the blood does leave our prefrontal cortex and we don't act rationally. A part of our brain that was developed much earlier takes over and we start behaving like reptiles. This part is programmed to help us survive, and causes us to fight or flee. This was pretty effective when we needed to escape a saber-tooth tiger but in most modern situations, neither fighting nor fleeing is effective.

Marriage researcher, John Gottman, of the University of Washington, found that when members of a couple become overwhelmed by their partner's negativity and their reactions to it, they go into systems overload or "flooding." According to Gottman, "We each have a sort of built-in meter that measures how much negativity accumulates during such transactions. When the level gets too high for you, the needle starts going haywire and flooding begins."

There are a number of strategies for correcting flooding. One method is to monitor our heart rate. The heart rate is an accurate barometer of the degree to which we are feeling overwhelmed and flooded. When one's heart rate climbs to ten percent above the resting rate, it's time to take a break or a time-out. It is extremely important to take a break if the heart rate exceeds 100 beats per minute. At that rate, the body is releasing larger quantities of adrenaline than normal and gets us into the dinosaur brain response of fight or flight or the Mad Guy response. Remember, too much blood in our hands, feet and tongue and not enough in our brain = STUPID!

What is interesting is that emotional stimulus can raise our heart rate as effectively as physical exercise. In one experiment, conductor Herbert von Karajan was wired to discover his autonomic response while he was conducting a symphony. The researchers found his pulse went up more dramatically during passages of emotional impact than in passages during which he exerted himself physically.

If you know you tend to become flooded with anger and anxiety in a heated exchange, you might want to buy one of the heart monitors on the market. These are available in athletic stores and are worn by athletes and exercisers to help them stay in a safe heart rate zone. Some are a bit unwieldy to have on for general conversation, but several are worn like wristwatches. The one I particularly like is a sports watch called the MIO. (Ordering information for this watch is on page 199.) When you are in an exchange that is becoming tense, you can monitor your own pulse. When you become aware that your heart rate is in the danger zone, it's time to take a time-out. This should be treated literally as a time-out where you leave the scene until your heart rate settles down. Once you are there, use a method of soothing your ruffled feelings until you are calm enough to resume the exchange.

There are several methods of soothing yourself, once you are in time-out. Here are a few:

1. Do deep breathing until you have calmed down. Breathe slowly and deeply, filling your lungs from the bottom up. Place one hand on your abdomen to monitor that you're doing it correctly.

2. Use self-talk while you are in time-out. You could say phrases like: "I am becoming calm and centered," or "These feelings will pass."

3. Some people feel calm enough to resume an anxiety-provoking encounter after vigorous physical exercise. Go for a run or a fast walk, or suit up and go to the gym for a workout.

4. Others respond to hydrotherapy. Get into a warm bath with bubbles or bath-oil and soak away your anger and anxiety.

5. Try the following exercise outlined by Donna Eden in her book, *Energy Medicine:* Think about the situation that has caused you distress. Hold it in your mind while you:

- Lightly place your fingertips on your forehead covering the ridges above your eyebrows.

- Place your thumbs on your temples next to your eyes. Breathe deeply.

According to Eden, in a few minutes this will bring the blood back to your neocortex and you will find yourself thinking more clearly. Then, calmly return and begin to solve the problem, using your 'human brain.' Learning to manage your emotions appropriately is a key characteristic of high emotional intelligence.

When angry, count four; when very angry, swear.

– Mark Twain

HEURISTIC

Find a way to soothe yourself that works for you and use it when you feel yourself getting out of control. You'll keep blood in your brain and take the smart action.

Complain Strategically

He that always complains is never pitied.

– Anonymous

My client Karen was a complainer. A charming, intelligent woman, she was often painful to listen to because she whined and moaned about the injustices the world insisted on wreaking upon her. Like Jarris in Heuristic Three, Karen had an inadequate sense of entitlement. The oldest of three sisters, Karen grew up with an autocratic and tyrannical father. His needs and desires prevailed. Woe betide the female in that family who didn't jump when Papa cracked the whip. One day Papa couldn't find his favorite cuff links. He threw a fit. Someone in the house had moved his cufflinks and they had better be found in a hurry or there would be dire consequences for all. The whole household dropped everything and for a tense half hour a thorough search was made. The cufflinks turned up in Papa's handkerchief drawer where he had dropped them. No apologies were made, none needed for an absolute monarch.

Growing up in such a household left Karen with an inadequate sense of entitlement. Survival for her meant putting others' needs before her own and never truly believing she was entitled to get her own needs met. Well, saints may be able to tolerate never getting their needs met, but those less developed souls among us know on some level that this is unjust. Some primitive survival instinct rears its head and wants to speak up. However, since it doesn't truly feel entitled, the only recourse is to complain.

There's a word for complaining more than once about something that complaining can't change: nagging. Complaining is also a big energy drain. It doesn't get results, it doesn't solve the problem and it seldom makes us feel better. However, it does have its place as a status quo maintaining procedure. This is how it works. Let us say we receive a psychic insult or injury—someone has hurt our feelings or done us an injustice. Some part of us believes we're entitled to something better. A little voice squeaks, "This isn't fair, I don't deserve this, this shouldn't be happening to me." This belief that we should be getting fair treatment clashes with the fact of our being treated otherwise and creates tension in us. If the tension builds up long enough, sooner or later something's got to give. One of four things will happen.

1. *The situation changes.* The person apologizes sincerely and makes amends. This is the one most desired, but least frequent.

2. *Nothing changes.* We endure and get backaches and migraines. This is the least desired, most frequent.

3. *We leave the situation behind.* Often not an option or an extremely disruptive one.

4. *We take authentic action and change the situation ourselves.* The only choice if we can't leave, we need the change and it isn't happening on its own.

Nearly all of us have discovered that if we tell our story (read *complain*) to a sympathetic third party who'll become somewhat indignant on our behalf, for a time we feel a little better. It really feels good to have someone say, "Awwww, poor baby." This causes some of the tension to abate, and then we can go back into the situation—still unchanged—and function.

The tension may have felt uncomfortable, but it also was an energy force that could have been used for change. Once it is reduced, the situation stays the same—the status quo is maintained. However, if the tension-energy is not siphoned off in complaining, it builds and builds until a critical mass is reached and the system changes.

So when you find yourself tempted to complain about something to a sympathetic friend, ask yourself: Do I want to reduce tension so I can stay in this situation or do I want to let the tension build so I can change it? If it's the former, by all means complain away. All of us complain from time to time and it feels good for a while. But if the situation needs to be changed, stop complaining, make a statement and take authentic action.

HEURISTIC

When you feel the need to complain, stop for a moment and ask yourself, " Do I want to be able to tolerate this situation that is unlikely to change or do I want to change it?

1. If it is the former, call up a sympathetic friend and explain the situation, asking if they will say when you finish, "Awwww, poor baby." Then take a deep breath and head on back into the situation.

2. If you want the situation to change, actively *don't* complain for a while. When the tension reaches critical mass, you will be able to take authentic action.

Be Willing to Live with Chaos and Confusion

Growth demands a temporary surrender of security.

– Gail Sheehy

M any of us have done this exercise in workshops on change: Cross your arms. Do it right now. Now cross them again the other way—the "wrong" way. Feels a little uncomfortable, doesn't it? Stay with the slightly "off" feeling it creates in you. Locate where it is in your body. That feeling is anxiety and you're experiencing a mild form of it right now. Can you hear a tiny voice squeaking, "Change back, change back?" This is what occurs when we make a change. The anxiety is so uncomfortable that we quickly run back to the old way.

Using a heuristic approach, you will try on new modes of functioning. This may feel uncomfortable at first. Change makes us uneasy because it throws us into a temporary state of disequilibrium. However, as Ray and Myers point out in *Creativity in Business*, "It is this very instability that leads to your creative responses. *Anything that increases the stress on the system leads to a jump to a higher state of being*" (Italics mine)—in other words, to a higher level of emotional intelligence.

Even small changes make us anxious. I've subscribed to the *Seattle Post Intelligencer* for all the years I've lived in Seattle. A few months ago they changed the font they regularly used to print the paper. They also changed key features of the layout to give it a new look. This is pretty simple stuff, but it has disturbed my morning routine. I look forward to having a pot of tea and reading the paper in the morning with the cat on my lap. My ritual was comfortable and predictable, and now it has been upset because the paper looks foreign to me. A simple thing like this is enough to make me feel the day isn't getting off to the right start.

If a tiny thing like changing the font in my daily paper can cause me discomfort, it's possible that some of the heuristics in this book will be similarly distressing for you. Knowing that in advance, you can understand that small anxieties have surfaced. Sometimes just knowing what is happening is enough, but if you need a little help, check out Heuristic Six, Learn to Soothe Yourself, and try out one or more of the suggestions.

The Dalai Lama believes that when everything seems to be going wrong all at once, something wonderful is attempting to come into being and is protecting itself by distracting us so that it can be born as perfectly as possible. If you feel at all uncomfortable with these processes, rejoice. Your new high EQ self is being born.

I'm all for progress, it's change I can't tolerate.
— Mark Twain

HEURISTIC

Be willing to tolerate the chaos, confusion and discomfort that sometimes accompanies change. Take action to soothe yourself if necessary.

Learn to Negotiate

Once you have learned what your non-negotiables are, life is simpler. Everything else is, by definition, negotiable. So now it's important to learn to negotiate. Unfortunately most of us didn't learn how to negotiate in the families we grew up in. We learned to manipulate, to demand, to whine, moan and complain. We learned to bludgeon, but we didn't learn true give and take in a relationship. Fortunately negotiating is a skill that can be learned. If we don't have well-established boundaries and we're not clear about our non-negotiables, true negotiation feels too much like giving ourselves away, so we go into automatic control mode whenever we feel anxious about getting what we want or need from someone else.

George and Sue had a problem. She wanted to sell their house and buy a bigger one, and he wanted to stay in the house they'd bought as newlyweds twelve years before. "Our mortgage would double, and we're barely getting by as it is," he said.

"But we have no room for our stuff," she countered. "We bought the house for location and because it looks good, but we forgot to accommodate our propensity to accumulate, and now we have nowhere to put anything."

They were at a stalemate and neither knew how to negotiate. They both had retreated into old modes of behavior that had worked for them in other settings. George, a giant of a man and supervisor of a construction crew, got his way by intimidation and by stonewalling any suggestion that differed from his. Sue, the youngest in a large, close family got her way by being helpless, and by complaining and manipulating. Neither had clearly established boundaries and both violated the boundaries of the other.

Both George and Sue were locked into their own *solution* to the problem. This was premature. We worked together to first discover the *issues*, and only then began to attempt solutions. It turned out that the issues for George were not taking on a mortgage that would be an onerous burden, and the comfort of staying put in an area he liked. Sue's issue was that the house had become so stacked they could never find anything, and she was embarrassed to have anyone over.

Then we worked on finding out where they agreed: Sue agreed that she was nervous about taking on more debt and George admitted the mess bothered him, as well. Once we became issue focused, the problem was fairly easy to solve. George looked into the cost of renting a storage unit and computed the cost of off-loading some of their accumulation to a rental unit, versus the cost of doubling the mortgage. It turned out to be a way for everyone to have his cake and eat it, as Sue, who was the worst offender, decided to reduce her inventory in order to keep rental costs down. Once they had separated boundary and control issues, the matter of selling the house or staying became a simple problem to solve.

Learning to negotiate is a must-have arrow in your quiver of relationship tools and is a great way to raise EQ. A good book to read for further information on the subject is *Getting to Yes* by Fisher and Ury.

HEURISTIC

When you are having a dispute:

1. Get clear on non-negotiables.
2. If this is a negotiable item, focus on issues.
3. Is there a solution that will serve both issues?
4. If not, settle on a compromise.
5. If you have trouble, call in a mediator.

Don't "Wear" Projections

Don't mind criticism. If it is untrue, disregard it. If it is unfair, keep from irritation. If it is ignorant, smile. If it is justified, learn from it.

— Anonymous

Everybody's got an opinion and they're entitled to it. However, a lot of folks feel compelled to share these gems of wisdom with us, particularly in the form of criticism. While we may not be thrilled to get this lovely data, we don't have to be shriveled by it because it is just that—an opinion. Let me share two examples with you. Two movie critics wrote the following about the movie *Persuasion*.

> *Whew! Sitting through 112 minutes of PERSUASION is a true exercise in persistence. Full of performances that could have been done better by hand puppets, sloppy direction, and a script that's nearly impossible to follow, PERSUASION has very little to redeem it.*
>
> *— Christopher Null*

*PERSUASION is a perfect movie. ... I have
never read it so the story was totally fresh. On
the other hand, this movie is so good that if I
had read the book a thousand times, it would
still have left me awe struck by the acting and
the production. I do hope all of the Academy
members see this show. It deserves awards in a
myriad of categories.*

– Steve Rhodes

Were these two guys watching the same movie? It's hard to
believe, isn't it? But they each brought who they are to the viewing and because of that, came away with such disparate opinions.
What was happening is a process called projection. Think of it as
a movie projector flashing an image on a screen. The screen is just
a blank waiting for an image. The image originates in the projector, which flashes its lights and shadows onto the screen.

Your critic is doing the same thing. Encumbered by the bag-
gage from all his previous experiences, your critic is predisposed
to see things in a certain way. Your song and dance, the way you
wear your hair, the meal you cooked, the report you wrote trig-
gered something in him from an earlier experience—yes, Dr.
Freud—often from childhood. And he projected this onto you in
the form of criticism.

An example: My husband hates bread pudding; I love it. When
he was a shy, bookish adolescent he went away to a boarding school
for the children of British military personnel where he was often
served a tasteless, gluey substance designed not to waste bread. To
him bread pudding represents poverty, loneliness and stinginess.
My bread pudding was made by my grandmother, who would
ensconce me in her kitchen with a cup of hot cocoa and tell wonderful stories about her childhood while she chopped nuts and

measured out raisins. The kitchen would be a little steamy, and the fragrance of cinnamon would permeate the air. Bread pudding to me is warmth, comfort and love. The bread pudding is the same stuff, but you can imagine the difference in our opinion of it. We have each projected our childhood experiences onto this humble dish.

Think of this the next time you find yourself reacting negatively to criticism. "Consider the source," my mother used to say. "Get curious," my therapist used to say. What do you know about this person that would incline her to such an opinion? Is this really about you or is this a projection? Is there some truth in what the person is saying? Is it a request for change dressed in the wolf's clothing of criticism?

If you can create enough distance to examine the criticism dispassionately, you can evaluate whether you need to make any adjustments based on this information, do so if necessary and then move on. There is no need to paint yourself in the color of the criticism. It is not you.

The best response to hostile criticism
is to yawn and forget it.

– Vladimir Nabokov

HEURISTIC

Listen carefully to any criticism. If it is unwarranted, acknowledge it for the projection it is and leave it behind. Learning to abide by our own internal standards is a way to develop emotional intelligence.

Accept Criticism for the Gift It Is

> *We should consider the person who shows our shortcomings as one who excavates a hidden treasure in us that we were unaware of.*
>
> – Venerable Henepola Gunaratana

I belong to a Toastmasters Club for professional speakers. One of the best things I get from this group is criticism. Luckily for me, they know how to do it right. They generally start out by saying what they liked about a speech—even when it stinks! Sometimes they really have to stretch to come up with something like, "I liked the way you didn't fall down the second time you tripped over the microphone cord" or "You only rendered me comatose for the first fifteen minutes of the story about your dog." Then begins the real stuff. "What I'd like to see next time is......." This is the gold.

But what if your critic doesn't do it that way? Well, sadly, most critics *don't* do it that way. Or do they? If we were not so busy wearing the criticism and getting defensive (see previous chapter), we could hear the unspoken part of their message, the part that says, "What I'd like to see next time is....." A request for change.

No one can change what has already happened, but a request for change is future oriented—let's do it differently next time.

We run into problems when both of us are projecting. Think of bread pudding. If you've spent your youth eating yucky institutional bread pudding and you criticize today's offering, you're projecting all that loneliness and stinginess onto the innocent dessert, or even worse, its creator. And if I grew up with a critical parent who terrified me when he criticized, my response to you may also come through the veil of that past experience and then *I'm* projecting. So here we are, both of us caught up in our previous experiences and we're calling it bread pudding. What it takes is for at least one of us to break out of that past pattern, get into the present and hear the request for a change in the future.

So how is criticism a gift? All of us in my Toastmaster's group are better speakers today than we were when we joined. The gifts we have received from each other as audience provide us with feedback on how to improve. Otherwise we'd keep repeating the same boring stories or making the same irritating gestures.

The heuristic in this case is to develop a pause button. Create a split second pause before you respond defensively to criticism to allow you to examine it thoughtfully. Is it a projection on the part of your critic telling you something about him? Or is there a gift nestling in the prickles?

HEURISTIC

When you are being criticized, pause and say, "Hmmm, let me think about that." If making the implied change will enlarge your life and /or improve your relationship, do it. And thank the bestower of such a lovely gift. The improvement raises your EQ.

Develop Your Sense of Humor

> *Perhaps we come to this planet for one great purpose: to develop a terrific sense of humor. Maybe laughter provides the key that finally unlocks the door to happiness.*
>
> – Dan Millman

B eing able to laugh at the serious situations life visits upon us and especially at ourselves as we flail around attempting to deal with life, is a mark of highly developed emotional intelligence. My grandmother used to say that life is too serious not to laugh at it. I guess she took life very seriously because she was an extremely funny woman. When I left Indiana to make my way in California and later Seattle, we carried on a lively correspondence. I loved getting her letters because, in addition to being loving missives, they were outrageously funny. I saved most of them and often read from her letters during my keynote addresses. Audiences really enjoy them and afterward tell me they wish they could have met her. Like all of us, she had her share of trials in life, but she managed to see the funny side of nearly everything. She was one of my best pacers. (See Heuristic Twenty-Four, Find Pacers).

There are a lot of pragmatic reasons for developing a sense of humor. For example, research shows that laughter reduces pain. One study found that subjects who laughed at a humorous video were able to tolerate more discomfort than a control group who did not watch it. In another study, a group of orthopedic surgery patients who also viewed funny videos asked for fewer tranquilizers and aspirin than a group of patients who watched dramas rather than comedy.

The ability to find the humor in what is essentially a tragic situation reduces tension and bad feelings associated with it. It's called gallows humor. In another study of humor, the researcher had her subjects view a film that featured three terrible accidents. One group was asked to tell about the film in a serious style, while another group was instructed to relate it in a humorous manner. The group who used humor experienced lower negative affect and tension.

There is also ample evidence that humor is good for our physical health. Writers on humor often cite the case of Norman Cousins, late editor of the *Saturday Review*. Cousins was hospitalized with a serious illness and not expected to recover. He decided to take charge of his own recovery, so he rented a hotel room and watched Marx Brothers movies and clips from the TV show Candid Camera and laughed himself back to health.

The best reason of all to develop a sense of humor is that it's fun. Laughing just plain feels good, which is reason enough to indulge in it. Just to give you a little smile, I include an excerpt from one of Grandmother's letters. In her last years she set up housekeeping with her son, my Uncle Bill. The two of them eked out a precarious existence on her Social Security check and whatever odd jobs Bill could come up with. Here's her tongue-in-cheek account of what must have been difficult circumstances:

There is mixed news on the financial front.
The good news is that your Uncle Bill got on a

crew at the cemetery digging graves. The problem with that is, he is paid on a piecework basis and no one has died in ages, so we have been pretty poor. Well, one did die last week, but they sent him over to Summitville. That just makes me so mad I could spit, as they never send us any of theirs.

But things are looking up. I was down at the Thriftway this morning and Zelma Ruth told me that Rol Fredricks is ailing and not expected to recover. Also, as I looked around, several of the citizenry looked on their last legs to me, so we'll no doubt be dining high off the hog before long!

If you are really lucky, you have someone like this in your life. Humorists tell us that we don't have to be stand-up comics to have a sense of humor. In fact, what is more important is to learn to see the humor in difficult situations and best of all to laugh at ourselves. Developing a sense of humor is one of the best ways to raise your EQ.

Human affairs are like a chess game: Only those who do not take it seriously can be called good players.

– Hung Tzu Ch'eng

HEURISTIC

Make a conscious effort to develop your sense of humor. Consider the positive payoff of learning to laugh at life. It will raise your EQ exponentially.

GETTING OUT OF MY OWN WAY

Often there are forces holding us back from developing our EQ. We will find the going easier if we first deal with these negative forces and get them out of the way. Only then will we have the wherewithal to direct our energies toward getting into the plus column of EQ development.

Get Rid of Energy Drains

If you are serious about being successful, start by eliminating everything you are putting up with, the things you are tolerating, enduring—those petty annoyances... Everything you are tolerating drains your energy, makes you irritable and wears you down.

— Talane Miedaner

The questionnaire for my high school reunion asked, "What are your hobbies?" I responded, "Finding my car keys." I was joking of course, but the truth is I've spent far too much of my life looking for those keys. When I come in the door my mind is racing ahead to the next thing: check my voice mail, check my snail mail, check my e-mail (are we starting to see a pattern here?). The car keys are part of the past. I don't need them now, so they fall out of consciousness and land—wherever—not to be thought of until I need them the next time. It has taken me an unconscionably long time to figure out there are better things to do with my life than be anxious because I'm running late and can't find the keys again. These three minutes or five or twenty-five I could spend looking out my window at beautiful Lake Washington spread out before me. And the anxiety saps energy that could have gone into alphabetizing my spice jars or something else really important.

Psychologist Kurt Lewin suggested that when we want to effect change, we analyze the forces both for and against change. He pointed out that the more efficient and effective method is to first get rid of the forces against change. What would be the forces against the changes we're tying to make in the direction of developing EQ? The answer is whatever is siphoning off our energy.

The problem is much of the time we're so stressed out we're not even aware of when our energy is seeping out. We are like my father's hands. My dad worked with his hands and they showed it. He was a tool and die maker by trade and spent many of his off-work hours tinkering with stock racing cars. I can still see his hands. They had grease rings around the nails that no amount of scrubbing would erase. The tip of the middle finger of his right hand was missing, caught in a fan belt of one of the cars. And the palms were so thickly callused that if he'd been a smoking man, he could probably have snuffed out his cigarette in his palm and not even have noticed.

Many of us have nervous systems that are as callused as Daddy's hands. We have become so accustomed to living with a high level of stress we don't recognize energy drains until they are huge. Energy is subtle. We are aware of the big changes in energy—the adrenaline surge when we receive good news, the sheer exhaustion of grief. But until we become more sensitized to it, we often don't notice the drain on our energy of the small leaks, such as being with a person who is constantly negative, the enervating effect of overriding our need for rest, or the loss of energy from rummaging through the rubble on our desks to find a missing paper.

Professional coaches tell us that we should make a huge list of all the energy drains in our life, and then systematically begin eliminating them. So we may come to them asking for help in attaining a goal of losing 25 pounds and attracting a new mate and be rather surprised by their advice to clear up the clutter in our office or drop a particularly draining relationship. Coaches have discovered Lewin's theory, first get rid of the forces against change. Only then will you free up the energy required to make the desired change.

What is there in your life that's a slow leak on your energy supply? Stuff around the house? There's a rug that's curled on one corner in our family room and every time I see it, I realize someone could trip over it. It's not big, but it's a drain. People can be this sort of drain as well. That's how we identify them— we feel drained after spending time with them. In fact they have siphoned off some of our energy supply to replenish their own low reserves. Sometimes this is what we do with friends—take turns sharing available energy—but some folks are chronic energy vampires. They never replenish your supply. We have a couple of choices here. We can face the problem squarely, set appropriate boundaries and keep spending time with them, or we can lessen the amount of time spent with those people. Identifying and getting rid of the chronic and acute drains on our energy frees us up to raise EQ.

> *To speed up ... you make one of two choices:*
> *reduce the drag or increase the thrust.*
>
> – Richard Handley

HEURISTIC

1. Make a list of all the energy drains you're dealing with on a consistent basis.

2. Systematically go through the list and divide it into two lists:

   A. Things I can do something about.

   B. Things that cannot be changed.

3. Tackle the A list one-by-one. For heaven's sake, put up a hook for those car keys.

4. Take another look at the B list. Are you sure? Is there anything you could move to the A list and then tackle?

5. Surrender the B list. (See Heuristic Forty-Four, Surrender.)

Clear Up Incompletions

I liken incompletions to holes in our water glass of life. Until these holes are filled (complete), one can never have enough water to keep the glass full.

— Thomas J. Leonard

Energy drains come in many forms. Unfinished tasks and projects deplete our energy in a big way. Keri can't go back to graduate school until she pays off her defaulted student loan. Jeannie and Ray know they need to make an appointment with an attorney and write their wills to protect their handicapped child. Joshua has a broken clock in the garage he's been meaning to get around to fixing—for the past 20 years! Incompletions are such a drag. They lurk back there somewhere in our sub-conscious and silently drain us.

Some of us are more prone to have a lot of incompletions around than others. It comes from a low need for closure. Research shows that about half of us have a high need to complete things and get them off our to-do list. My college professor Dr.

Charlie Seashore says jokingly that checking things off their lists is as close to a sexual experience as these high closure-niks ever come to. Of course, Charlie's a low closure kind of guy, himself.

The other half of us are great starters, but poor finishers. We tend to begin things with great enthusiasm, but when the project hits a snag or goes on for too long, we put it aside in favor of the next exciting idea. The problem with this unfinished business is that it takes up space, physically and psychically, slows us down and robs us of energy, all of which holds us back from developing our potential emotional intelligence.

Finishing one of these projects feels like we suddenly weigh less—the weight on our shoulders has been lifted. A few years ago my mother started knitting an afghan for me and then broke her finger about two-thirds of the way into the project. She said her knitting fingers never felt right after that, so it sat in her closet for a year or so. Finally, when I was on one of my trips back to Indiana to visit her, she insisted I bring it home with me. I was faced with the choice of finishing it or getting rid of it. Now, I can do a sort of rudimentary knit and purl, but I'm no knitter, and this was a pretty complex design. But I could not bring myself to get rid of it, so it sat in the bottom of *my* closet for many more months.

Personally, I have only a moderate need for closure, but every time I looked at that unfinished throw, it nagged at me. Finally I asked my knitting friend Eva for advice. I was actually hoping she'd take the project on, but she didn't take the hint. I guess this demonstrates we should ask directly for what we need! (See Heuristic Twenty-Four, Ask for What You Need). Instead she designed a simple knit and purl pattern that even I could follow. I got in the habit of working on it while I watched TV and taking it with me on car trips, and after several months, I got it finished. It felt great. I didn't have an orgasm over it, so maybe Charlie exaggerates a little, but it was wonderful to get that project completed and it looks marvelous draped over my couch.

As long as something is around to nag you, when it stays on your mind or comes up as a reminder or feeling, it is an incompletion. Clear these up and plug energy leaks.

HEURISTIC

Make a list of your unfinished projects. Estimate the time it will take to complete each one, then double that time. Trust me on this. Then set aside several blocks of time devoted to one project at a time and get it done. Get it out of your hair, off your mind and check it off your list. Alternatively— decide not to complete it and get rid of it. Who knows, maybe you'll have a sexual experience.

Give Up Addictions

> *Addiction involves compulsively seeking to use a substance, regardless of the potentially negative social psychological and physical consequences.*
>
> – Mayo Clinic

I'm addicted to ice cream. I admit it. Whenever I have it in the house, I am ill at ease until it's gone. It calls to me in the night. "Jeanne Anne," it croons in a voice as smooth and creamy as Placido Domingo's, "here I am, waiting for you. Come and get me." I'm also addicted to a confection called Poppycock, a luscious combination of popcorn and nuts in a butter-toffee coating. Its voice is scratchier, more like Rod Stewart's or Louie Armstrong's when it calls. Having these things in the house creates a tension in me that is only eased when they are gone, and I can't believe I ate the whole thing!

I don't mean to make light of addictions. They're no joke. Most of us have addictions of one kind or another that range from mildly troublesome to outright deadly. Telling someone to give up cherished addictions is one of those things that is simple to say but difficult to do.

One theory of addictions is that they manage anxiety. Many of us have a higher tolerance for the pain of maintaining our addictions than we do for the anxiety we would experience if we gave them up. According to the anxiety management theory, we become addicted when we discover by trial and error a substance, an activity or a person that for a time masks our anxiety. This becomes our Drug of Choice (DOC). The reason it only works for a while is that it doesn't hit the sweet spot. It is band-aid therapy, which only covers up the anxiety. It doesn't deal with its cause, so we continue to need more and ever more of the DOC.

We probably need help to get rid of serious addictions. The Alcoholics Anonymous program has been successful for a great many people who were unable to do it on their own. There are also treatment programs that have been successful. This is not new information for anyone with an addiction that is seriously undermining their life. But there's no way to get in the plus column toward raising EQ when these chains are holding us back. Get whatever help is necessary.

HEURISTIC

Get out from under the addictions that are holding you back from achieving your potential. Get help if necessary.

16

Simplify

> *I meant to lead a simple life, to choose a simple shell I can carry easily—like a hermit crab.*
>
> – Anne Morrow Lindbergh

Ken can't throw anything away. He grew up in a household where waste was a sin. "You never know when you might need it," was his mother's frequent refrain. The anxiety he experiences at the thought of tossing anything out causes him to keep all manner of stuff in the vain notion that he'll find a use for it someday. As a result his house is only days away from being like the apartment of the nutty uncles in the movie *Unstrung Heroes*, with paths through the maze of magazines and stacks of newspapers he can't bear to part with. "The biggest problem, aside from having no space for anything, is that I know if I needed one of those articles or gimcracks I pick up at garage sales, I'd never be able to find it," says Ken. Still, he hangs on. "You never know…" Ken needs to jettison some cargo and simplify his life.

I also have a difficult time letting go of things. I hang onto things long after they have outlived their value to me. It seems that after I have invested part of myself in them, in longing for them, eventually acquiring and then using and taking care of them, it's a waste to get rid of them when they're no longer useful. I think that somehow, if I try harder, if I look longer, and if I turn over just one more stone, I'll find the answer to regenerating value in this thing (person, project, size ten pants). But hanging onto useless articles, people or situations when they no longer have value is another of those things that sap and seep our energy.

The recent proliferation of books on simplifying life tells us a chord has been struck that resonates down through our over-busy, over-stuffed lives. A few years ago my friend Patty found herself divorced at age 45. Her children were grown and established in homes of their own and she gave most of her things to them, keeping the bare essentials to live in a tiny, furnished apartment. She wore a uniform to work so needed few clothes. "I can pack everything I own in the world into two cardboard boxes," she said ruefully.

Instead of hearing this as a sad state of affairs, I found myself yearning to reduce my inventory. To have to keep track of, polish, repair, sort, clean, and store only two boxes of stuff. What would I keep? My kids' baby pictures. A treasure or two. How would I pack my piano into one of the boxes? What about the cat? Does she count as a possession?

Needless to say, I didn't pare down quite so drastically, but I began to think in terms of simplifying. How to have as little as possible so that I have everything. What is everything? How much is enough?

Sometimes thinking of simplifying our lives feels a bit too much like depriving ourselves. After all, we work hard and feel entitled to the things we have acquired. It may be helpful there-fore, to think of increasing the 'pleasures' we have in life, rather than acquiring more and more 'comforts.' Comforts are those things that make life easier or take less effort, such as dishwashers, air conditioners and microwave ovens. Having these doesn't make one happy, but having had them, we are *un*happy when one of them breaks down and we must go without it. Pleasures, on the other hand, are experiences such as flowers, good food, music and conversations with friends. Without these, we're not necessarily unhappy, but having them definitely brings happiness. The French and the Italians spend proportionately far more of their income and energy on the latter than most of us do in the United States.

Alix Kates Shulman, author of *Drinking the Rain,* went to live in an isolated cabin in a Northeastern state. She said her aim was to pare down and pare down until she found the least amount she could do with and still be happy. How little could you have in order to have everything? What is the least amount it would take in order for you to be happy? When we are not encumbered by our possessions, we unleash energy that can be used in ways that bring us more satisfying pleasures.

> *Manifest plainness,*
> *Embrace simplicity,*
> *Reduce selfishness,*
> *Have few desires.*
>
> – Lao-Tzu

HEURISTIC

Ask yourself these questions with each new bit of stuff, with each new project, each new something that wants to intrude on your time and space, "Will this enlarge my life or clutter it? Will the happiness units I get from this outweigh the cost units to get and have it in my life?" Simplifying frees up energy, which raises EQ.

Give Up Perfection

The perfection lies deep within your
imperfection. Embrace your cellulite.

– Molly Jong-Fast

I am one of those people who have bought the myth that I ought to be—well, different from how I actually am. I really believe I ought to be thinner, richer, nicer, more successful and happier than I am—in other words, perfect. I also think the people around me should be perfect, or at least a heck of a lot closer to it than they currently are.

Things are supposed to go right, too. Cars are supposed to start on cue and never have batteries that give out on you on a rainy day when you've parked head-in with cars on either side of you and no one can get close enough to give you a jump. Feeling this way makes me cranky.

Here's how I'd like to be instead. I'd like to have a good laugh at my expense when I'm hemmed in with a dead battery and just go on back in to wherever I came from, have a cup of coffee and wait until one of those cars leaves and I can get a jump. I'd like to have people over and not think I have to first clean up the stacks of papers and books that clutter our living space. What I do now is stash stuff in grocery bags in the closet and then forget I did that and later can't find anything. The inconvenience of it all keeps me from having people over as often as I'd like. It's really dumb because I'm not fooling anybody. All my friends know this about me. And anyway, whose friends love them because their house looks as though Martha Stewart is in charge? Of course, if I were perfect, as I should be, I wouldn't have those stacks in the first place.

I've decided to have a role model for the kind of laid back, contented, easily tickled person I'd like to be. I don't know anybody like this in real life, though I think they're out there. They probably avoid uptight types like me because we haven't got our priorities straight and they don't like the vibes we give off. So I'm having to imagine her.

I've named her Annie, which was my childhood nickname. Annie's a little older than I am, a little overweight and she has let her hair go gray. Annie's comfortable about herself; she doesn't get upset over small things she has no control over and she seems to easily forgive herself when she screws up, which is about as often as I do. She also laughs it off pretty easily when those around her screw up. She eats as much ice cream as she really wants. It's funny, I've noticed she doesn't eat as much of it as I think I'd eat if I let myself do that. Maybe that's what happens.

Annie thinks a whole lot of things are amusing or downright hilarious, especially herself when she doesn't quite manage it all. She says, "If you don't hit what you're aiming for, consider what you hit as the target." That's pretty profound coming from somebody as down-to-earth as Annie, but sometimes she surprises you.

Here's my homework assignment for myself. I'm working on raising my consciousness about this, and whenever I catch myself getting uptight about something I ask myself what Annie would do in a similar situation. I'm getting there. The other day a friend dropped over unexpectedly. As we were chatting I noticed her gazing in a puzzled way at something, and when I glanced over to where she was looking, I saw a sock on the mantelpiece. I just smiled. I know Annie would.

HEURISTIC

Give up the need to be perfect and become more accepting of yourself and those in your life. If you need someone to show you how, you're welcome to use Annie. She won't mind.

DEVELOPING RELATIONSHIPS

Relationships are where it's at if we are in the business of raising our EQ. Discovering who we are, and maintaining that self in the midst of people who are important to us is the essence of EQ development.

Holding Onto Yourself in a Relationship

*Someone may be a fool and not know it—
but not if he or she is married.*

– H.L.Mencken

I once heard someone say, "When you live alone, all your bad habits disappear." It's true. When you're by yourself, no one cares if you pick your nose or wear tatty underwear. The process of living with another person is a real soul tumbler, grinding off our rough edges and making EQ diamonds of us. It's one of the most intense graduate courses in raising emotional intelligence.

The book, *The Bridges of Madison County*, and the movie based on it, were both highly popular. The story involves a lonely, married woman who meets a romantic stranger while her husband is away. The two immediately recognize each other as soulmates and are caught up in an intense romance that lasts four days in real time and the rest of their lives in mind and memory.

That story struck a chord because it represents a yearning we all have for someone who could "know" us in the deepest sense and love us unconditionally forever. The real problem with stories like this is they give us hope that this is possible without the rest of the 'stuff' of relationships. Of course, I'm talking about the bad habits that get on each other's nerves, like her propensity to talk too long on the telephone, and his habit of cutting his toenails in the living room and leaving the clippings on the rug. But even more, I am talking about the way we try to avoid developing ourselves and instead find someone who will complete the part of us that is missing and between us make one whole person.

When this is the case, as it is most of the time, we may start off with blissful togetherness and play our own version of *Bridges of Madison County*. But once we get past those four days (weeks, years) of untrammeled ecstasy, trouble starts. The problem is, we have projected half ourselves onto the other person, and then we get anxious because we've given over control of that part to the other person, who doesn't handle it properly. Actually we were anxious in the first place and passed the hot potato over to the other person in hopes they'd cool it off for us and lower our anxiety. When it doesn't happen—which it doesn't because it can't—the relationship starts to unravel.

The paradox is this: in order to improve our relationship, we must first work on ourselves; we must raise our own EQ so that we are mature enough personally to be in a mature relationship. Developmental psychologist Erik Erikson said that an individual is available for an intimate relationship only after he or she has achieved a core sense of identity. Of course, he was talking about a person having developed emotional intelligence.

This is counterintuitive. It really does seem as if it is the other person causing the problems. It is so easy to see the transgressions of the other party, and so nearly impossible to have such clarity of vision about our own part in the turmoil. But, it's the bad news and the good news. We have to do the work ourselves; that's the bad news. The good news is we *can*. I have no control over you so

I can't do your work for you, but I can control myself so I can do the work that's called for on my part.

The payoff is, as we develop our emotional intelligence, we get better at relationships. When we work on self—finding out who I am and what I want—and taking responsibility for our own emotions, we automatically become more sensitive to the emotions of the other. When we are aware of our non-negotiables and calmly take authentic action when necessary to maintain integrity, we do not feel reduced or shriveled when we give to another. When we are not giving ourselves away, we are then in a position to love someone else wholeheartedly and do all that we can to help them. Being in a close, loving relationship ranks high on the list of heuristics that develop EQ.

> *Did I pick the right person? The universe hands us a flawless diamond in the rough. Only if we are willing to polish off every part of ourselves, do we end up with a soulmate.*
>
> – Hugh Prather

HEURISTIC

Allow yourself to be in a relationship without losing yourself. Allow your rough edges to be buffed in the process. This is EQ development at its most intense.

Hang Out with Kids

> *I have found parenting to be the most powerful teaching of any teacher I've ever had, and I honor my teachers very deeply.*
>
> – Judith Lasater

If you really want to develop high EQ, have a child or adopt one or two—or six! Everyone knows parents aid in their children's development, but it is less known that children contribute to the development of their parents. You learn a lot about yourself when you are up all night with a child screaming with an earache.

My sister Sue had children before I did. At the time, having just graduated from college, I was an expert on raising kids. Like the truly generous person I am, I freely shared my expertise with her, tactfully pointing out where she was going wrong and helpfully suggesting ways she could improve on her parenting. Then I had a humbling experience: I had kids of my own and immediately lost my expert status.

We know the pendulum of human development swings between the opposite poles of developing self and developing relationships. When I am developing self, I'm learning who I am and what I'm good at. I'm learning what I want and what

I'm willing to put into getting what I want. Self, self, self. It's all about me.

When I'm developing relationships, I sometimes put what I want on hold for a while or give up getting some of what I want in order to help you get what you want. Parenthood is an exercise in developing relationships taken to its extreme. When we're parenting, we put our own needs on hold so long it sometimes feels as if the other party hung up while we were busy finding clean socks.

Mothers especially have traditionally submerged a self in the aid of their children's development, but in recent years, more and more fathers have begun taking an active role in raising their kids. Research tells us this is good news, indeed, for our kids, as children do better in all aspects of their lives with increased involvement on the part of their dads. This is also good news for all those dads who are busy raising their own EQ in the process, and good news for us if we have to deal with them.

When the children are babies and toddlers, their needs seem endless, but most of the time we forgive them because they so clearly have no understanding beyond their own needs. Also, they're cute and helpless and they arouse in us a need to take care of them and love them. And then, inexorably, they become teenagers and *really* tax our ability to stay the course, maintain ourselves and put our needs on hold. Novelist Fay Weldon said, "The greatest advantage of not having children must be that you can go on believing that you are a nice person. Once you have children you realize how wars start." Something tells me she was dealing with teenagers.

Sue Miller, another novelist, speaks to our exquisite need to maintain ourselves when our children are being their most unreasonable selves—when we need to stay the course, utilize our human brain and be our most emotionally intelligent. Miller writes,

*Having children teaches you, I think, that love can survive your being despised in every aspect of yourself. That you need not collapse when the shriek comes: **Don't you get it? I hate you!** But you do need to get it. You do need to understand and accept being hated. I think this is one of the greatest gifts children can give you, as long as it doesn't last.*

Raising children calls upon us to be at a stage of development few of us have reached when we are in our childbearing years. Biology demands that when we have children, women, at least, are of an age when they have not yet faced the major life situations that sand us off and make high EQ people of us. This means part of our children's development comes from learning to deal with imperfect people—their parents—who are still working on fairly early stages of their own development.

This may not be an altogether bad circumstance for the kids. English psychologist, D.W. Winnicott said that what children need are "good enough" parents. He believed that if a child could have a "perfect" parent, he would not be prepared for the vagaries of the real world.

Probably one of the reasons the relationship between grandparents and their grandchildren is easier than the parent/child relationship is, in interacting with their grandparents, the children are dealing with people who are at higher stages of EQ development than that of their parents.

What can you do? Roberta Gilbert, author of *Extraordinary Relationships,* says, "Of all the legacies a parent can give children, by far the best is that of raising his or her own level of differentiation (read EQ) as high as possible…. If that is the parental focus, the children will automatically function better."

So it's a win-win situation. In the process of raising children, the kids win by learning to deal with people who are essentially immature themselves. We win because our rough edges are buffed off as we put our needs aside to attend to those of the kids. Raising the kids automatically raises our EQ, which makes better parents of us. And putting a true focus on raising other aspects of our emotional intelligence, makes us still better parents.

> *How on earth can anyone bring a child into the world knowing full well that he or she is eventually going to have to go through seventh and eighth grades?*
>
> – Anne Lamott

HEURISTIC

Have a child, adopt a child, become a foster parent, become a Big Brother or Big Sister, or become a volunteer baby-sitter for friends who have children. Spending time around kids is a true EQ raiser.

Ask for What You Need

Ask and it shall be given you.

– Matthew 7:7

Pat and Sam, a couple in their early 30s, were having another of their "theme" arguments. Like most couples they squabbled about a lot of different things, but when we looked deeper into the conflict, we usually came up with their theme, what family therapists call their "core affective issue." Our instructors in family therapy training told us, "When it could be the title of a country western song, you've found the core affective issue." The song for Pat and Sam was, *"If you really loved me, you'd know what I need and give it to me."* Pat sang this to Sam with theme and variations.

"You never bring me flowers or give me back rubs," she accused him during a session in my office.

"I do, too give back rubs."

"Only when I ask you to. You never volunteer."

"You mean he does rub your back when you ask him to?" I interjected.

"Well, yes, but I'd like him to do it of his own volition once in a while," responded Pat.

"Does it feel good to get the back rub, even though you had to ask for it?" I persisted.

"Of course, but why doesn't he see once in a while that I need something like that? I can usually tell when he's down and needs some sort of a lift. Why can't he be as sensitive to my needs?"

"In other words, you're a pretty good mind reader, and you want him to be one, as well?"

Pat is not so different from most of us. It would feel wonderful to have someone so attuned to us that they'd instinctively know what we need and give it to us without our having to ask. Good luck! There aren't many of those gifted psychics around. Most of the time, if we want to get our needs met, we need to ask for what we want and be explicit about it.

It works in the opposite direction, as well. Sometimes we're busy following the Golden Rule, treating others as we would like to be treated and feeling it's not appreciated. Kathy and Juan are a case in point. Kathy grew up in a large, noisy family who easily expressed their affection for one another. Kathy loved Juan a lot, so she planned his fiftieth birthday party like a war campaign. She invited fifty of their "closest friends(!)" There were balloons with mushy notes in them and people reading funny tribute poems. It was a great party. Just what Kathy would've wanted to feel loved and appreciated. She was devastated when Juan finally confessed he would rather have had a quiet dinner alone with her to celebrate.

Juan grew up in a family where they expressed love and appreciation by doing things for each other. Kathy had been complaining that their kitchen was too dark. Juan loved Kathy a lot, so for her birthday he bought her a chainsaw, climbed the tree in the back yard and excised the offending branches. The kitchen's a whole lot brighter now, but Juan was devastated when Kathy didn't like his gift. Juan and Kathy need to be clearer with each other about what hits the sweet spot for them and then ask for it. They also need to ask for this information from each other. Since I can't read your mind, what would do the trick for you?

Are you feeling under-appreciated at work? What would make you feel appreciated? Flowers? A handwritten note from the boss? A round of applause from your coworkers? Get clear on what would hit your appreciation button and ask for it. Do you feel you're giving more than you're getting from your main squeeze? What would right the balance? A special dinner cooked the way you like it? A contribution to your collection of antique beer coasters? Ask for it, directly. As I write this, it occurs to me that I would feel more successful as a speaker if I got a standing ovation for my efforts. I'm going to request this from my Toastmasters Club.

HEURISTIC

Get clear about your needs and what would fulfill them. Ask directly for what you need. And then express your appreciation.

Learn from Difficult People

I have learned silence from the talkative, tolerance from the intolerant, and kindness from the unkind; yet strange, I am ungrateful to these teachers.

– Kahlil Gibran

The whiner, the steamroller, the know-it-all, the passive aggressor. Oh how we'd like them out of our lives. They enrage and frustrate us. They drive us crazy. Why don't we just herd them all together, give them plane tickets and ship them off to their own island where they can't bother anyone but each other? Well, we'd better not, because most of us would be standing in line with a boarding pass. But an even more important reason is that difficult people are precious mines of self-knowledge for us.

Not long ago I conducted a seminar on *Coping with Creeps: How to Deal with Difficult People*. Those of us in the room, naturally enough, were the good guys. The difficult people were those poor excuses for human beings outside the room. Then we all took the *Myers-Briggs Type Indicator (MBTI)* and got familiar with our personality preferences and, lo and behold, we discovered some of those difficult people sitting right next to us. Difficult people, it turned out, were people who were different from us. And we found that *we* were difficult people to *them*.

For example, some of us felt punctuality was supremely important—a sign of consideration for others and a way of making the world function more efficiently. Others had the notion that time is nature's way of making sure everything doesn't happen all at once, and figured that if we arrived sometime within the same decade, we were on time. I had the groups divide and talk to each other about this issue of punctuality. Soon it became clear that if your notion of time is different from mine, we are each going to be a difficult person for the other.

A simple rule in dealing with someone that is hard to get along with is to remember that this person is striving to manage his anxiety. If we keep this in mind and deal with him from that point of view, we will find these dragons a little easier to tolerate.

The most effective way to deal with difficult people is to learn to style-flex. That is, find out what their style is, and for the transaction you are having, be flexible enough to step momentarily into their style of doing things. So if this person likes to schmooze a bit before getting down to business, your response should be to relax and chat about the family. If, on the other hand, the person is brisk and efficient, cut to the chase, get to the bottom line and stop wasting their time. You'll be more effective and these difficult folks won't seem quite so difficult.

The second thing to do with difficult people is to consider them a gift. Medical intuitive Carolyn Myss says that we all have made a spiritual contract with the people in our lives and that we should love the difficult ones the most. According to Myss, these folks love us so much that they have agreed, according to the contract, to make our lives difficult and even to endure our hatred and contempt in order to teach us the lessons we're supposed to learn. If you have a hard time wrapping yourself around such a concept, read Heuristic Forty-Six, Suspend Disbelief, and operate as if it were true. What do you care, so long as it makes your life better?

Judy had been married to a real steamroller. Life in the marriage was extremely troublesome for her, as she didn't have very well developed boundaries. Years after she left him she learned to be grateful to him for teaching her the importance of establishing and maintaining boundaries. Now when she bumps up against one of these intense controllers, she isn't even fazed. She says, "When you've lived with the toughest son-of-a-gun in the valley, these other folks are wimps." Had she been married to someone more easy-going, she'd still have fuzzy boundaries and those steamrollers would be hard for her to deal with.

If we had our choice, we probably would never choose to spend time with difficult people. The heuristic of learning from these ornery cusses is a sure way to jump several steps higher on the EQ scale. But it can be stressful, so be sure to take care of yourself in the process and give yourself periodic breaks from dealing with them.

We have met the enemy and he is us.

– Pogo

HEURISTIC

Get curious about the lesson you are learning in dealing with difficult people. You're really high on the EQ scale when you can see them as the gifts they are. Or you could buy them a plane ticket.

Learn to Take 'No' for an Answer

You can't always get what you want, but if you try sometime, you may just find, you get what you need.

– The Rolling Stones

My stepsons, Joe and Bob, lived out of state when they were young, and visited us during their vacations. They were very strange kids. Sometimes they would ask me normal kid questions like, "Jeanne Anne, can I eat a *Three Musketeers* bar for breakfast?" or "Is it okay if we put the cat in the clothes dryer as a scientific experiment?" Of course I turned down these charming requests. Frankly, I was surprised they asked first, but this is what really blew me away. I would tell them no and then brace myself for what was to come. *Nothing did!* They would simply shrug, say, "Okay," and go on back to their video games. I really liked that about them. Of course I realized they were developing abnormally, but these kids had learned what a lot of adults haven't: they could take 'no' for an answer.

Before I had my step-kids, I raised two *normal* kids. Naturally, kids feel freer to be their real selves with their parents than with anyone else, so I got the usual cries of outrage and the barrage of reasons why I should change my mind from Lance and Katy when I said no to them. Katy told me later that she could remember how her body felt at times when she got a negative response to a request. "I felt as if something was growing and burning inside me and that I was going to explode if I didn't get what I wanted," she explained. I think that's what's going on inside all of us when we don't get what we ask for. We're burning alive, ready to explode.

To gracefully take no for an answer is a way of respecting another's boundaries. One of the hardest things about being appropriately assertive is that we are going to have to say no to someone who might not like it. And of course, it works both ways; when we hang out with people who are appropriately assertive, sometimes they're going to say no to our requests. When they are defending their emotional acre, we must respect the boundaries they have established.

What do we do then with the anxiety that comes up as a result? How do we respond when our bodies are going to explode? We recognize what's going on, hit the pause button and learn to soothe ourselves. (See Heuristic Ten, Soothe Yourself). Consider it an opportunity to develop your EQ, as it really buffs off our rough edges when we don't get what we want and we have to find a way to live with it. And the Rolling Stones may be right, we may be getting just what we need for our development when we don't get what we want.

Sometimes God says no.
– Author Unknown

HEURISTIC

Learn to be gracious when a request is refused. You are respecting the boundaries of another when you gracefully take no for an answer. Learning this is a wonderful way to raise EQ.

Communicate Responsibly

Communication of ideas is dependent upon an emotionally calm brain state for reliable thought production.

– Roberta Gilbert

Working with parents and teachers is part of the job of a school psychologist and often one has to communicate bad news to them. Most people do pretty well with it, but from time to time we encounter those who are just plain difficult. These people quickly get a reputation in the school district and most of us try to avoid them if we can. But Cathy has a magic touch with these folks. People who have given nearly everybody in the school district a bad time will come out of her office smiling and being cooperative. Her boss once called her "Silver Tongue," thinking she had some way of fast talking these people into a change of attitude. "I don't have a silver tongue," she explained, "but I hope I have Golden Ears." Cathy's secret is simply that she is a world-class listener.

Most of us feel we are good listeners because if we were stopped in the middle of an exchange we could probably parrot back what the speaker just said to us. We might have heard the words, but as Cathy says, "We have missed the music." The difference is, when we merely hear, we may know what they said, but when we truly listen, the other party *feels* as if they have been listened to. How do we create this feeling? We manage ourselves during the communication process and listen actively, rather than focusing on the answer we're formulating.

Often what gets in the way of good listening is our own anxiety about what the speaker is saying. When we feel as if a basic need—maybe even a non-negotiable—is being threatened or compromised, our anxiety starts to rise and the music beginning to play in our heads is much louder than the spoken words. No wonder we can't hear what the other is saying.

It's easy to listen to what the other person is saying when we don't have a lot invested in the outcome but when we are in an emotionally charged situation, the picture changes. There's Velcro all over the place and it's easy to get stuck to the emotionality. When this is occurring it is necessary to process our own anxiety. This is the time for maintaining and self-soothing. (See Heuristic Ten, Soothe Yourself.) It's no easy task to unhook from this morass of feelings, but if we are to be optimally effective in the interchange, it is a must.

Sometimes it seems as if we should process all these negative feelings with the one who conjures them up in us, but this can have the effect of burdening the relationship with more emotional intensity than it can tolerate. It's easier on the relationship if we process these feelings on our own. This is perhaps the ultimate in taking responsibility for our own feelings.

HEURISTIC

Learning to process your own anxiety in the communication process improves relationships. Learning to take responsibility for our own feelings is a good way to raise EQ.

GETTING A LITTLE HELP FROM FRIENDS

Most of the time we have 20/20 vision about what the other person in the relationship is doing. But where we are concerned, we sometimes need some help to "see ourselves as others see us," as the poet, Robert Burns wrote. We also need people to set the bar a little higher, and people who influence and motivate us to be our highest EQ selves.

Find Pacers

One evening's conversation with a superior man is better than ten years of study.

– Chinese Proverb

My friend Daneen is a dynamo. Bristling with energy, she is also young, gorgeous and very bright, in addition to being lots of fun. Daneen is a highly capable person who has not let her youthful appearance get in the way of her running a successful business. She has a full therapy practice and a thriving practice as a corporate consultant, in addition to writing a regular column for a large metropolitan newspaper. She also has a handsome husband and a darling baby daughter.

Daneen is one of my pacers. I look at her in wonder and think I should be doing all she does, but our styles are so different there's no way I could do what she does in the way she does it. But as I see her, I know I can adapt some of what she does and do it in my style. Because she's in my life I extend myself. I see possibilities I wouldn't see on my own.

I have a number of pacers in my life—folks that are a step or two or a whole staircase ahead of me. They show me the way. They demonstrate that it can be done. Fellow students were pacers who saw me through the doctoral program. Tobe bushwhacked a trail and Alice set a breathless pace. By panting along in their dust, I managed to finish my degree.

My husband, Terry, is also one of my pacers. He's the smartest person I know, and that's saying a lot, as I've administered over a thousand IQ tests in my career. After he retired from his job as a computer software engineer, he took up residence in the local library—well almost. At his peak he had 92 items checked out, books on every imaginable subject. Being around all this erudition keeps me on my toes. After all, I need to try to understand what he's talking about.

My friend Yvonne is a spiritual pacer. She has endured losses and catastrophes that would send most of us into a deep depression, including the death of a grown son, nursing her husband through a long, eventually fatal illness, and braving health problems of her own. Yet, I've never seen her off-center. She has a spiritual core that sustains her and makes her an inspiration to those around her.

Lee, my smart cousin, is often dismayed that he seems to be constantly surrounded by so many who are below his level of intellectual development. I tell him that if he's the smartest person in the room, he's hanging out with the wrong crowd. If we are consistently in the company of people at a lower degree of development than we are, we may feel superior and it may massage our ego, but we don't grow. Oliver, a championship tennis player, says, "Always play with a better player than yourself. It is how you get better."

HEURISTIC

Surround yourself with pacers, with people who are smarter, better educated, more highly developed, more spiritual and/or more accomplished than you. You will stretch yourself to keep up with them and in the process, automatically raise EQ.

Join a
Support Network

When I tell others what my goals will be, knowing they will be brought back in writing to the next meeting, I'm motivated to accomplish them!

— Alice Rowe

My Master Mind group meets at 7:00 AM on alternate Thursdays at Tully's Coffee Shop on Capitol Hill in Seattle. This means I get up at 5:30 to avoid rush hour traffic so I can get there on time. Why on earth would a night person like me do something like that? Because we are a group of people on a fairly similar quest, and we support each other on the journey. The six of us provide each other with encouragement, accountability, resources, ideas, referrals, advice and a listening post. All this for the price of a double-tall, skinny, split-shot latté (we talk that way in Seattle) and a cinnamon-raisin bagel.

A growing number of people are discovering the power of joining with like-minded people with the intent of helping one another be successful—however each individual defines success. Management literature calls these groups Success Teams, Advisory Boards or Empowerment Teams.

One group has the following mission statement:

- to support one another in achieving our stated goals and help each of us to become successful professionally and financially;

- to assist each other in staying focused, take meaningful steps and meet commitments;

- to listen carefully to one another without judgment;

- to share insights and feelings in a supportive manner; being responsible for asking for what we need. (See Heuristic Twenty-Four, Ask For What You Need)

- to make one another feel challenged as a way of moving forward; and

- to share ideas for resources toward personal and professional development.

This group starts its meetings with a short meditative period where the members listen to music, answer a question or just sit quietly. This is followed by a five-minute check-in for each member, sharing the News and Goods (or Bads) that have occurred since last meeting. After this comes group time during which each member requests what he or she needs from the group, which may be a brainstorm for a title of a book or workshop or a critique of marketing or training material. Next comes goals and accountability. How effective have I been in meeting the goals I set last meeting and what are my new goals. These are written down for each member and brought back to the next meeting. How much harder will I try to keep a promise to myself if I know that my comrades are going to question me if I don't?

HEURISTIC

Form or join a Master Mind group. There is power in such a group. The energy exchange will rev you up into a higher gear and in the process of having your feet held to the fire, you will grow your emotional intelligence.

Find a Mentor

There are three ways to get to the top of a tree: 1. climb it; 2. sit on an acorn; or, 3. make friends with a big bird.

– Robert Maidment

What big bird could make a difference in your life? I've been lucky to have a number of important mentor relationships. Several able school psychologists served as my big bird by taking me under their wings and showing me the ropes of the profession when I was a fledgling. It would have taken me many more years than it did to learn such a complicated job without their help. Later, when I chose to become a speaker, I once again had mentors who helped me cut through the complexity of the speaking profession.

As organizations flatten, there are fewer people to serve as role models for those who come up behind. This places more of the responsibility for people to educate themselves back on their own shoulders. One way to do this is to develop a relationship with a mentor.

Daniel Levinson, who studied the development of adult males, found that a mentor relationship was one of the most important a person can have in early adulthood. A mentor may fulfil any of several roles, including those of teacher, sponsor, host and guide. A mentor can provide counsel and moral support when times are stressful. Mentors can also be role models for the kind of person we would like to be. The most critical role of a mentor is to provide support and to facilitate the realization of the mentee's goals for the future, especially what Levinson called, "the Dream." A mentor encourages the development of emotional intelligence in his young protégé by believing in the younger person, sharing in his or her dream, giving it his blessing, and creating a space in which the younger person can create a life structure that contains the dream.

If you could have anyone you wanted for a mentor, who would it be? From your perspective, who embodies the person you'd like to become? Who has achieved what you'd like to achieve? Once you've identified a prospective mentor, ask yourself, "Why would this person want to mentor me? What would be in it for him?" When motivational speaker, Albert Mensah was just beginning his career, he identified a successful speaker and offered to come to one of big bird's presentations at his own expense and to make himself useful in any way he could, passing out handouts, ushering and selling products for big bird in return for some coaching and feedback. He not only received mentoring, big bird called him up to the podium and introduced him as an upcoming star, which proved to be a real boost to his career.

"But," I can hear you saying, "I'd be afraid to ask big bird. She's so successful and so busy she wouldn't have time for the likes of little ol' me." Good. I'm glad you recognize that. It'll keep you from being a pain in the neck, but don't let it get in the way of asking. Even if she turns you down, she'll be flattered you asked. And you'd be surprised at how often a prospective mentor will take you up on your request, if you follow a few simple guidelines.

- Make it clear that you recognize the limitations on their time and that you'll be respectful of this by not asking a great deal of this precious commodity. Negotiate for a specific amount of time and then stick to it. Don't make the mentor be the timekeeper.

- Offer something in return for being mentored. What chore could big bird pass along to you that would enrich his life or make it easier in some way?

- Be aware of what you want to learn. Don't leave this to the mentor; it's your responsibility.

- With big bird's help, set goals and establish a deadline by when you are to accomplish them.

- Do your homework. Nothing is as frustrating to a mentor as an overdependent mentee who doesn't take responsibility for her own learning.

Having a mentor is an excellent way to help us develop our emotional intelligence.

> *Keep away from people who try to belittle your ambitions. Small people always do that, but the really great make you feel that you, too, can become great.*
>
> – Mark Twain

HEURISTIC

Identify someone you'd like for a mentor and make it worth their while to help you. Then follow the guidelines for successful mentoring.

Get Into Therapy

All things being equal, the life course of people is determined by the amount of unresolved emotional attachment, the amount of anxiety that comes with it, and the way they deal with this anxiety.

– Murray Bowen

It's really hard to go forward when there are compelling forces holding us back. Sometimes it's hard to tell what's getting in our way without an outside observer. Friends and family are too close to the subject and may not respond in a way that is helpful to you. A therapist can give unbiased feedback and help figure out the best ways to solve problems. A therapist can also help when we are trying to negotiate a major change in our lives, and we need help managing the anxiety so that we can stay the course.

Most of us have issues from our past, which we think we've left behind us, but which may be getting in our way today. Laura came to me because she thought she must have a strange magnet that attracted people with a particular set of irritating personality traits. Everywhere she went, she kept running into these people and they were driving her crazy. "Of course," she said, "they do just what my mother used to do to me. Am I fated to go through life surrounded by these people?"

Laura wasn't really surrounded by these people; it just seemed that way. She made a list of all the major players in her life and was surprised to discover this type was definitely in the minority. But when she ran into one of them, it was a major energy drain for her because they were able to push her buttons in a big way. She was unable to maintain herself in the face of this much anxiety.

What was happening was like painting with watercolors and your brush is too wet. Let's say you've just painted a yellow flower and you're starting on the green of the leaves when you get your brush too close to the yellow that's still wet. What happens? The flower is now chartreuse. All it took was a drop of green to change the whole flower. When we have unfinished issues from the past, we are a still-wet yellow flower running around vulnerable to a green brush. It only takes a drop and suddenly we can no longer maintain our color.

Perhaps the issue was a highly critical parent who was able to shrivel our self-esteem. If we haven't resolved this issue, we're vulnerable to anyone who is critical of us. One encounter and our self-esteem is in the basement. And it feels as if the world is filled with folks who do this, when in fact, they are just the ones for whom we have the Velcro. They toss, we catch and it sticks.

A therapist can help lay these ghosts. Family and friends may be sympathetic, but they're too close to us and have too much invested in a particular outcome that may or may not be in our own best interest. A therapist is trained to be neutral and can help figure out the best way to work through the issues.

Getting into therapy is a scary prospect for many people because they imagine they'll have to wade through a mire of pain that is best left alone. "What I don't know, won't hurt me," said Lynette, after yet another broken romance. The problem was that what she didn't know *was* hurting her a lot. She kept trying to work out issues from the past in the current relationship. It kept going wrong because she was seeing today through the glasses of yesterday and had a distorted view of what was going on. Getting into therapy turned out not to be as painful as she imagined it would be and not nearly as painful as repeating her same old mistakes.

Our anxiety about making changes keeps us stuck in the pain of the current situation. A therapist can be an adviser, a cheerleader and a guide, helping us see our way through and, like a birth coach, reminding us to breathe when we feel overwhelmed by our anxiety. Getting help when we are dealing with issues from the past is one of the best ways to raise emotional intelligence.

HEURISTIC

If you have unfinished issues from the past, stop letting them get in your way and raise your EQ by finding a good therapist and working through to an effective solution.

Hire a Coach

It (coaching) is a professional relationship with someone who accepts nothing but your best and who will advise you, guide you, and encourage you to go beyond self-imposed limitations in order to realize your full potential.

– Talane Miedaner

Ancient wisdom says when you're ready the teacher will appear. Until then consider hiring a personal or professional coach. A therapist helps you settle issues from the past that are getting in your way. A coach looks in the opposite direction and helps you identify and reach your goals for the future. People who want to accelerate their growth hire a coach to help them get there. According to Talane Miedaner, author of *Coach Yourself to Success,* "Coaching closes the gap between where you are now and where you want to be."

A coach "hears" between the lines and helps you realize what you really want out of life. Then you begin a process of getting rid of the small annoyances that drain energy, clearing the field so that you can set appropriate goals. At the same time, you begin to add activities that give you pleasure and thus increase your energy. A coach will hold you accountable—perhaps the most important task of all. Sometimes we make promises to ourselves, but then life or old habits get in the way, and we conveniently forget the promise. But if we had someone to report to, we might not forget. A coach helps us fish or cut bait. Either lose that ten pounds or accept yourself the way you are. Either write the book or put your efforts into marketing your business.

One of the reasons we give up on a goal is that it seems so large or so far in the future. A coach can help you break a goal into manageable chunks and keep encouraging you when you hit the inevitable snags. Coaches help you stay the course when you encounter these speed bumps. Rather than abandoning a project that has encountered problems, we can see it through to the finish with the support we get from a coach.

Some coaches work on the theory of attraction. It works like this: We've all been told that the way to get what we want out of life is to set goals and find a way to go after them. This can lead to our trying to force our way through to the goal and can result in frustration. When you use attraction, you work on becoming the kind of person that attracts your goals to you. The way to do this is to systematically remove the energy drains in life in order to create a vacuum that will cause the good things to rush in to fill the space. In other words, as we work on raising our emotional intelligence and getting the right smarts, we will automatically attract the things in life we want in order to be happy and successful.

HEURISTIC

Find a good coach to work with. Give it at least three months and then evaluate where you are at the end of the 90 days compared to where you were at the start of the collaboration. This is a guaranteed way to keep you out there on the edge and raise your EQ.

DEVELOPING SELF

It is a paradox that when we develop our intellectual and technical abilities, the process raises our EQ. When we focus on education and training and on seeing the world in new ways, we transform ourselves.

Be an Education Junkie

Go back to school. Get a degree if you don't have one. Get another degree if you do. Or don't bother about a degree. Go back to school not for credit. "But I'll be 35 (45, 65 or even 85) by the time I get the degree." So what? Remember what Ann Landers says, "How old will you be in four years without the degree?" I was 51 when I started back to school for my doctorate. I tell people that unlike more modest types, I *want* people to call me by my title. I got the degree so late in life, I'm afraid it won't get all used up unless people call me 'Doctor' a whole lot. My husband gets to be less formal. He calls me 'Dr. Honeybunch.'

Socrates studied music in his later years. He was asked, "Aren't you embarrassed to be studying in spite of your age?" Socrates is said to have replied, "I would be more embarrassed to be ignorant in spite of my age." The idea behind this thinking is that if we're older when we start, we won't have enough years to work at the new profession to justify the time and money spent to obtain it. Well, certainly vocational preparation is part of education, but a less acknowledged, equally important purpose of education is to promote development. In other words, to raise EQ.

Earl Shorris, social critic and author, believes that education in the humanities transforms the lives of the poor and disenfranchised more than the "point A to point B benefits of job training." He started the Bard College Clemente Course in the Humanities, a program offering college-level courses to the poor. Lyall Bush, director of the Seattle branch of Clemente offers the poetry of Tess Gallagher and T.S. Eliot, art history, Greek theater and the philosophy of Hobbes to street people, dropouts, recent immigrants and recovering alcoholics. Bush believes that education raises EQ, though he doesn't phrase it that way. He says, "You walk in and you come out different on the other end."

Education improves people's lives in several ways. According to Bush, the humanities can push people to self-reflection and give them a lever with which to move the world. The people who stay the course begin to see the world in a new way. If education—especially education for its own sake that is not directed in a straight line toward vocational training—can do this for street people, it can work for all of us.

Education is also a form of brain insurance. A new study demonstrates that a lot of education, both formal and informal helps protect us from the confused thinking that affects many people as they age. According to the study, people with a lot of education can operate without memory loss or thinking problems despite a surprising amount of brain shrinkage.

Another benefit of increased education is that it raises the level of our moral development. At lower levels of moral development, people do the "right thing" because there is someone around with the power to make them do it. At this level, someone finding a purse with identification in it would only turn it in if someone were there who had the power to insist on it. Higher up on the rung of moral development, people do the right thing simply because it is the right thing to do. Their conscience has grown. One study looked at the factors that went into raising moral development. Education won hands down. People with more education demonstrated higher levels of moral development than those with less education.

Education doesn't have to be formal to count. My grandmother, with an eighth grade education, was extremely well read. And these days it's easier than ever to education oneself. A world of education is no farther away than your local library or your home computer.

Development is the fundamental aim of education.

— Lawrence Kohlberg

HEURISTIC

Become a lifelong learner. Begin today to get more education and never stop. This ranks high on the list of developmental spurs that raise EQ.

Upgrade the Quality of What You Read (and Watch)

> *Habituate the self to the humanities, for from them and in them are seen the wonders of thought and the subtleties of reflections.*
>
> — Aristotle

There is a book exchange in a small store not far from my house. You can bring in two books and take out one of comparable quality. The problem is, there's not much of any 'quality' to trade for. The vast majority are *popular* as opposed to *literary* books. I'm not sure how the distinction is made or who makes the choices, but for me it's like the judge deciding about pornography, "I recognize it when I see it."

I certainly read my share of trashy novels, but after a time they pall and one wants a book to actually say something. Author Fay Weldon says,

> *The good (writers), the really good (writers), carry a vision out of the real world and*

transpose it into the City of Invention, and refresh and enlighten the reader, so that on his or her return to reality, that reality itself is changed, however minutely.

Weldon is telling us that reading good literature raises our EQ. In her book, *Letters to Alice on first reading Jane Austen,* Weldon writes letters to her fictional niece, Alice. Alice has complained that she was required in a college course to read Jane Austen, whose books she found "boring, petty and irrelevant." Like most of us, Alice turns to television or easy reading, popular books for most of her stories. And like most of us, Weldon, herself, admits to suffering from "the common nervous dread of literature." She says her practice while on vacation is to first read thrillers, then sci-fi, followed by instructional books. Only then does she reluctantly and with some dread pick up *War and Peace,* which one *ought* to read, and then is carried off in "the kind of swooning, almost erotic pleasure that a good passage in a good book gives; as something nameless *happens.*"

The difference between good literature and popular reading is that great literature is developmental and the popular stuff just fills time. Nobody grows, changes or develops in any serious way and neither do we as a result of our exposure. When we read good literature, we end up knowing more about ourselves. Weldon says, "You do not read novels for information, but for enlightenment."

The same principle applies to movies and TV. The films that move us or touch our hearts are those in which the characters develop. In the process of wrestling with the problems or obstacles they encounter, the characters come to view the world differently and then change their behaviors. They grow more emotionally intelligent. In the movie *Marvin's Room,* for example, the Meryl Streep character enters full of scorn for her self-sacrificing sister who has passed up marriage and a family of her own to stay behind and look after elderly relatives. By the end of the movie, the Streep character comes to understand that her sister may have the more enlightened view of life, and thereby starts her own growth process. And in watching it, so do we.

Read good books.

– Kenny Walden

HEURISTIC

Begin to upgrade the quality of what you read and watch. Ask your librarian or bookstore manager for suggestions. A great way to get started is to listen to the books while you're in your car. Many great books are now on tape. I've listened to almost all of Jane Austen driving back and forth to work. The readers are so good at dramatizing the books that you can almost fool yourself that it's a trashy novel.

31

Keep a Journal

There comes a journey and there also comes the urge to write it down, to bear witness to our experience, to share our questions and the insights that come from questioning.

— Christina Baldwin

I've kept a journal for over twenty-five years, but I'm not faithful at it. I tend to write when I'm going through a difficult period in my life. When life is good, I don't seem to want to do it so faithfully. If I died tomorrow and my journals were discovered, I'm sure those who read them would believe I'd led a sad and troubled life.

Since I *don't* write more often than I *do* write, I suppose that means I'm happy more than I'm sad, which is, in fact, the case. But when I'm in trouble, I write a lot. I filled whole volumes during the period just before, during, and after my divorce, one of the worst times in my life. And this is what it did for me. After a few weeks of writing I would go back over what I'd read and I could begin to see patterns. Issues that came up over and over began to clarify. Once I could define a problem, I was on my way to solving it. Human dilemmas are not always easy to pin down.

It's difficult to see the dimensions of the problem. As we write day after day, it's as though it sets off something in the back of our brain that works and works when we may not be aware of it, until one day the pieces fall into place and we can see our way clear to a solution.

Writing helps us discover what we really feel. It also helps us combine memories from the past with present experience and put both into a clearer context. This helps us come up with creative solutions to current problems and helps us come up with new approaches to old problems.

Writing helps us use both sides of our brain in problem solving. When we are under stress, we tend to fall back on whichever is most comfortable for us. If we tend to be right-brain types who typically see the whole picture, under stress we may overlook important details. Conversely, if we tend to be left-brainers who are attentive to the small pieces of a situation, we may, under stress become bogged down and paralyzed by the details. Writing helps us use both parts of the brain. It brings up the images, feelings, hunches and connections that come from the right brain and slows us down enough to use the left brain to make logical sense of these images and helps us create strategies and solutions.

Sometimes people write letters in their journals. You could write letters to yourself—to the self you will be when you are 80 and looking back on your life, or to the five or ten-year-old you were when life was spread out before you. A journal is also a place to write letters to other people—to those dead and alive, to those in past and present relationships. Most of these will never get sent, and in fact, shouldn't be. That's not the point of this type of letter. This is another way of taking responsibility for our own feelings in a relationship and working them through on our own. Once the emotion has been processed, we may choose in a calm, respectful way to share these with the other party, or we may discover there is no necessity to share this at all.

Julia Cameron in her book, *The Artist's Way*, suggests doing what she calls morning pages. This is writing three pages every morning first thing on awakening—before the coffee's brewed or the cat's let in. Especially before your conscious brain kicks in to direct and judge what you write. You certainly have greater access to unconscious material this way. Keeping a journal helps us to develop insight, to see situations and people in a new light. It is this growing and changing that is the essence of development.

There are other benefits to writing about our experiences. A recent study shows that patients with chronic illnesses experienced a reduction in physical symptoms when they wrote in a journal for 20 minutes, three days in a row about emotionally stressful incidents. Earlier studies have demonstrated that writing can relieve tension and improve immune functioning. Keeping a journal not only raises EQ, it helps us keep a record of our growth.

HEURISTIC

Begin today to record your thoughts in a journal. Be open to the discoveries you make as you write and as you read over what you have written before.

Learn a New Skill

You can't teach an old dog new tricks.

– Ancient aphorism

We've all heard the one about the old dog not being able to learn new tricks, haven't we? As it happens, learning new tricks may be what keeps the dog from getting old before its time. It's a use-it-or-lose-it situation. Brain research tells us that as we learn new skills, we open up new pathways in the brain, helping it to make new connections.

It's really frustrating at first, especially when we're older, to be new at something again—to start at the beginning. After a long, successful career as a school psychologist, I began a new career as a professional speaker and author. It has been difficult to go from being the 'expert'—the one who knew the ropes and who trained new interns—to being the new kid on the block who has none of the answers and doesn't even know all the right questions. Had I known how much there was to learn, I might've found it too daunting to start, but the process has been fun and enlightening, as well as difficult.

The subskills that go into learning a new skill carry over into other aspects of our lives. Self-discipline, persistence, patience and a tolerance for frustration are useful tools to have no matter what we're doing. And as we know, staying just outside the edge of our comfort zone is one of those buffing devices that grows EQ.

Probably the best reason to learn a new skill is just the pure enjoyment of using it. Ben picked up the flute his son had abandoned years before and decided to take lessons. Now he plays in an amateur orchestra that meets once a week and sometimes serenades nursing homes and other organizations. He's no James Galway, but he says he's having a wonderful time.

I've been learning Spanish for the past few years. In our class we joke that we're learning a new language at an age when we're having trouble remembering the names of our own kids. We figure we're losing English at about the rate at which we're acquiring Spanish, and in a year or two we'll be monolingual again, but in a whole new language.

HEURISTIC

Learn Thai cooking, learn to speak Swahili, dust off the bassoon in the closet and learn to play it. The heuristic is to learn to do something new. *And enjoy it!*

Travel

> *If there's a choice between putting $2,000 in an IRA versus $2,000 in a trip to the North Pole to see if Admiral Perry's footprints are still there, I'd say, " Go to the North Pole," because that will awaken the world around you, and their interest in you, and you'll learn a lot more from it.*
>
> – Michael Phillips

The first time I traveled in a foreign country I went with someone who knew the language and customs where we were going. I put myself in his hands and it was great fun. He went back home, but I stayed on to attend a conference. For the four days between his departure and my arrival at the conference, I was on my own. What an education! Suddenly things I took for granted back home were huge obstacles to overcome: making a phone call, catching the right bus, figuring out the money, ordering breakfast. They say travel is broadening. This may be because you can't read the breakfast menu posted in the French café and there's a basket of delicious croissants in front of you and you eat them all because you don't know how to order anything else. Maybe it's your rear end that broadens when you travel.

Even going to the bathroom was an ordeal. I never knew if it was going to cost money, if I had the right change or whether I could locate the critical handle, chain, knob or button. There were also expectations for women's behavior, especially women traveling alone. By the time I came home, I looked at life in a whole new way.

A trip to a third world country made me realize I'm incredibly rich. I have electricity, running water and an oven. I even have a car. This is wealth beyond imagining to Claudia, the maid who cleaned our hotel room and who is rasing three children without the benefit of any of these things. My friend Lynda travels frequently to a town in Mexico. She discovered that many children live near the dump just outside of town, and scavenge there in hopes of finding any scraps from the castoffs that would help them survive. Lynda now is active in a program that provides relief to these kids. Be aware that traveling may raise your consciousness as well as your EQ, and you may find yourself involved in ways you can't imagine. I've included contact information on page 199, if you want to contribute to the Children of the Dump project.

Traveling also teaches us about ourselves. When I'm on the road, I am always struck by how narrow my physical comfort zone appears to be. I think of myself as a pretty tough old bird, but I find myself fretting if I'm not within the temperature zone that's comfortable for me—I don't want to be too hot or too cold. The bed I'm sleeping on may be too hard or too soft. I feel like Goldilocks looking for the one that's just right. I either have to learn to adjust or be miserable.

It's important to stay curious and flexible when we travel. Too often Americans want it both ways—we want the comforts we are accustomed to, but we want to climb the Leaning Tower of Pisa, as well. If money is no object, we may be able to accomplish both. Certainly most places in the world have American-type hotels to stay in and these days, there's a McDonald's nearly everywhere. But we miss something essential when we try to duplicate the world we left. Last fall my husband and I traveled to Ireland so he could show me his birthplace. We could have stayed in American-style hotels, but we would've missed Irish breakfast and the landlord's beautiful, brand new baby daughter, Aisling, had we not stayed in the charming bed and breakfast we chose in Killarney. Travel is definitely transformational.

HEURISTIC

Travel, especially to foreign countries. It helps us get outside ourselves and see another way of viewing the world. This automatically raises EQ.

Go Against Type

The more we mature, the more our non-preferences add richness and dimension to our lives.

         – Otto Kroeger & Janet Thuesen

Are you a chatty extravert who never meets a stranger? Or perhaps you're a shy, retiring type who's most comfortable alone or with a few well-known friends. Do you like to plan your day carefully ahead so you know what to expect or do you prefer to stay loose, keeping your dance card open for whatever turns up? All of us have preferences about the way we behave and given a choice, we stay with our preferences. However, stepping across the line to do the opposite action will be more growth producing for us than staying with the old comfortable methods.

I often start workshops on personality types by having people write their names. Try it now. Just write your name on any piece of paper—the back of an envelope will do, you won't have to turn it in for credit. Now write your name with the other hand. What was it like the second time? Unless you're ambidextrous, you probably found the second time more difficult than when you wrote with your dominant hand, and you're probably not as satisfied with the results, right? But you were able to do it, and it's probably legible. This is what happens when we go against type.

I'm not proposing that you switch to your non-dominant hand for your writing chores, although it's probably helpful to do that once in a while. (See Heuristic Forty-One, Do Neurobics). What I am proposing is that you become aware of the way you customarily do things, and try to do it from an opposite approach. For example, if you love occupying center stage at a gathering, try giving the floor to someone else and remaining mostly quiet for the duration. If you usually wait for others to initiate contact with you, be the first to speak up and say hello. Then check your reactions.

Most of us feel a little anxious when we go against type. The people who like to have their day pretty well lined up in advance are managing the anxiety they experience when they encounter unplanned events. They like to be well prepared and feel uncomfortable when they don't have things in place before an event occurs. And those who prefer to field whatever comes at them feel tied down and anxious when their day is too well planned. After all, what if something better turns up?

What I am suggesting is that you do the opposite of what you usually do and learn to self-soothe when the anxiety arises. (See Heuristic Six, Soothe Yourself). The purpose of this exercise is to develop our undeveloped parts and help us become more rounded individuals who can better handle whatever life chooses to throw at us.

Imagine taking a car trip to Nowhere, Nebraska. Some of us would get on the Internet or call AAA and get the trip planned out in detail. We'd know how far we were going each day and have reservations at our various motels. We'd get the car serviced, stop the paper delivery and pay all our bills in advance. Others of us who prefer more spontaneity in our lives would just get in the car, get out on the freeway, find another car that looks like it might be headed for Nowhere and follow it. The first way sounds comforting. There'd likely be no unpleasant surprises, but it seems a bit confining and doesn't allow for much in the way of discovery. The second approach sounds adventurous and exhilarating and certainly you'd wind up somewhere, but it might not be Nowhere. That may be the more exciting way to travel, but what if you needed to be in Nowhere?

Another activity would be to do the opposite of what you usually do in terms of scheduling your time. If you look at your date book and can't see any white space because you schedule yourself so tightly, try having a non-scheduled day once a week and don't wear your watch. Let your natural rhythms have a chance to take over. If, on the other hand, you tend to stay loose and handle whatever comes up, try a page out of the over-scheduler's book. Schedule your activities and follow the schedule closely for a period of time. I guarantee that this will be uncomfortable at first, but you'll find out how the other half lives and learn something about yourself at the same time.

By operating exclusively in one mode, we lose out on the offerings of the other modality. By going against type we learn to gain the benefits of both. And we raise our emotional intelligence as we grow.

HEURISTIC

Become familiar with your type and preferences and, from time to time, switch for the opportunity of experiencing it in a different way. You'll stretch yourself and grow your EQ.

Be Flexible

Balance the day with poetry and play. To overcome the danger of rigid patterns of behavior, break the order of the day with disciplined wildness.

– Ronald S. Miller

Children below junior high age have a difficult time with *what if.* For example, say you're explaining to your seven-year-old that he should fasten his seatbelt, and he wants instead to stand up in the back seat and be free of restraints. You say to him, "What if we were to stop suddenly? You'd be thrown out through the windshield." Your young one points out reasonably and logically that you're a careful driver and you are not going to make a sudden stop. In his experience, this has never happened and he is unable to conjure up the possibility that it could. He may comply, and he may even parrot back your reasons, but he truly won't be able to imagine what *isn't.*

Around junior high age, kids begin to be able to hold two opposing views at the same time. Beginning somewhere in adolescence, your child may be able to see that it is reasonable for him to want to take the car for the evening and that it is also a valid point that you need to be at a meeting and must have the car yourself. He may press his point vociferously, but he can at least understand there are two equally valid truths at issue. This is the beginning of flexible thinking.

Some of us revert to this childishly rigid way of thinking when we get older. Rigidity is often thought of as what occurs in older people, but it's actually a reversion to earlier ways of thinking. It's going backward.

Yoga increases our physical flexibility. As the body is stretched and twisted in yoga postures, blood, lymph, and—according to practitioners—life force is allowed to flow into previously restricted places, keeping joints and hinges oiled and allowing full range of motion. The same thing happens when we keep our minds flexible—allowing new data in lets us examine several viewpoints at once.

Staying flexible helps us when we're in a conflict. We can get truly curious about the other's position and perhaps alter our own as a result of the new information we're taking in. When we stay rigidly locked into our position, nothing can get in. The life force can't flow and we have a reduced opportunity to come to an agreement that is satisfactory to both parties.

Gregg Levoy in his book, *Callings,* suggests that being stuck in a particular position, being fixated on something amounts to a loss of soul. When we stay locked in place we are subject to becoming "overwhelmed by the downward-pushing forces that govern all moving bodies—gravity and inertia," according to Levoy. He recommends the arts as a way of leading us toward movement, toward a more flexible, creative outlook. Cultivating a flexible mind is an excellent way to raise EQ.

HEURISTIC

Staying flexible in our thinking is a way to let in the new data that allows us to keep raising EQ. Consider breaking the order of the day with a little disciplined wildness.

Be Persistent

When nothing seems to help, I go and look at a stone cutter hammering away at his rock perhaps a hundred times without as much as a crack showing in it. Yet, at the hundred and first blow, it will split in two, and I know it was not that blow that did it, but all that had gone before.

– Jacob Rils

Stasey, a 32-year-old single mother of two, received no child support and was having trouble making ends meet in her dead-end clerical job. She decided that the way to solve her difficulties was to get more education. "I'm going to go back and complete my degree and become a teacher," she excitedly told me in her counseling session. "It's the only way out of this dilemma." We sat quietly after this pronouncement and I wondered. The road ahead would be difficult and Stasey's pattern was to begin a project with great enthusiasm and then, after hitting the inevitable difficulties, she would give it up, only to start another project with equal excitement. Stasey's problem was, like many of us, she wanted things to be easy, and when they weren't, she abandoned them.

The opening words in M. Scott Peck's book, *The Road Less Traveled*, are "Life is difficult." I feel my stomach tighten just a little when I read those words. I don't want it to be true, but of course, it often is. Most of us don't want to deal with difficulties. I'm no exception. I'd like to just go for my goal and achieve it without all the sweat and toil and certainly without all the interruptions, mistaken assumptions, unanticipated costs, errors, blind alleys, and people problems that are snags along the way.

We get into trouble when we expect no problems. Then when they arise, we feel overwhelmed and often give up. If we expect from the beginning that problems will arise, we can shrug our shoulders, tighten our resolve and get on with it when they show up. It's like bringing an umbrella along in Seattle, even when the forecast is sunshine. It wasn't supposed to rain, but since it has, we're prepared and we aren't going to let it deter us from our plans. Henriette Anne Klauser, author of *Write it Down, Make it Happen*, says we should treat problems we encounter along the road toward our goals as speed bumps, not roadblocks.

I wanted to help Stasey gain a realistic perspective on her new endeavor, without discouraging her from going for her goal. "What will you do when it gets hard?" I asked her.

"What do you mean?"

"I agree with you that this is a wonderful, and maybe even necessary step for you to take, but have you given any thought to what you'll do when difficulties arise?"

"I don't want to think about that. If I do, I'll be too scared to start," she replied.

"Of course I don't want to scare you off, but let's make some contingency plans. Then if you really do encounter hardships, you'll have something in place so you don't have to stop."

Together we brainstormed and came up with a list of all the ways her plan could go wrong. Then we brainstormed solutions to each of the possible problems, trying to come up with as many as possible for each situation. Of course it could happen that none of the problems we thought of would occur, while a host of others we hadn't envisioned might lay ahead. The point of the exercise was to allow her to expect problems, to identify them as such and because most problems have a solution, she could take them in her stride and find ways to solve them, instead of caving in to her anxiety and assuming that an obstacle was a sign she never should have undertaken the enterprise.

The story has a happy ending. Stasey went for her goal and actually saw it through to the finish. She did encounter several of the problems we predicted and a couple we never dreamed of, but because she knew to expect them, they only increased her determination. She is now in her second year as a kindergarten teacher in a large suburban school district.

Never give in, never give in,
never, never, never, never.
– Winston Churchill

HEURISTIC

Expect problems and obstacles to erupt when you undertake something important to you. Then find a way to go around or through them and keep on keepin' on.

Do Neurobics

> *Neurobics makes the brain more agile and flexible overall so it can take on any mental challenge, whether it be memory, task performance or creativity.*
>
> – Lawrence Katz & Rubin Manning

Remember crossing your arms the 'wrong' way in Heuristic Twelve? Try it again now. Experience the strangeness of it. This is another activity that keeps us just outside the edge of our comfort zone, but it turns out that simple things like this can keep our brains sharp. Doing exercises such as taking a different route to work, driving with mittens on or switching seats for home meals gives the brain the novelty and multisensory experiences it needs to keep a keen edge. Lawrence Katz and Rubin Manning describe activities like this in their book, *Keep Your Brain Alive.*

Katz and Manning call such activities "neurobics," which are a synthesis of recent brain research findings. Engaging in neurobics nudges the brain awake and stimulates its "attentional circuits." This starts the flow of growth-promoting molecules known as neurotrophins. When the brain is stimulated by novelty and experiences that engage the emotions and at least two of the five senses, the brain produces these neurotrophins and creates new circuits that improve memory and boost logical and creative thinking.

A bonus for senior citizens is that neurobics can reduce the decline in brain functioning that inevitably occurs with advanced age. The popular belief is that mental decline is a result of the unavoidable steady death of nerve cells. Instead, it is the thinning of the number and complexity of dendrites that is responsible for mental decline. When we engage in novel experiences, especially when they are paired with sensory stimuli, the brain is more active than when we perform familiar routines. New dendrites are created, which act as pathways in the brain. According to the authors, "The aging brain ... continues to have a remarkable ability to grow, adapt, and change patterns of connections." This is good news, indeed, for anyone interested in developing emotional intelligence.

HEURISTIC

Wear earplugs to breakfast, get into your car and start it with your eyes closed, sniff vanilla or peppermint first thing in the morning, brush your teeth with your non-dominant hand. Or buy Katz and Manning's book and try all 83 of the neurobics they suggested. Better yet, give your brain an even more rigorous workout by thinking up your own neurobics.

DEVELOPING THE BODY-MIND CONNECTION

The connection flows in both directions—mind to body and body to mind. The effect each has on the other is profound and cannot be overlooked if one is to develop a high level of emotional intelligence.

Take Care of
Your Health

Anna, an older friend often says, "God, just give me health. I'll take care of the rest." She understands that it's difficult to feel any joy in life when your body hurts. You've heard it all before so I won't go into it in any detail here. It's simple. We just have to live like the Geritol lady in the commercials a few years ago—eat right, get plenty of rest, exercise, take your vitamins and don't smoke. The Geritol lady didn't mention this, but it also helps to have methods for appropriately dealing with stress. That's it. It's not rocket science.

It's not that living a healthful lifestyle in itself develops emotional intelligence, although exercising discipline and learning to tolerate current pain for future gain is a way of raising our EQ. But in the matter of staying healthy, it's more that the alternative holds us back. When we are sick, the energy units we might use in a positive direction are being deployed in an effort to maintain the organism and regain health.

It's really so simple, but simple doesn't necessarily mean easy, especially in this culture. We are bombarded with conflicting messages all the time. Pick up any women's magazine. On succeeding pages you will find articles about how to lose weight and get in shape, followed by advertisements for cake mixes and recipes for diet busting goodies. We're urged to get off the couch and exercise, while at the same time we're flooded with electronic ways to avoid ever moving at all—we don't even have to get up to answer the phone or change the TV channel any more. It's no wonder that obesity is reaching crisis proportions in this country.

It helps to have company in this effort. I have a tendency to be a sofa tuber, myself. I'm a great reader and given a choice, I'd much rather curl up with a book than work out at the gym or take a five-mile walk. I'm lucky to have my husband, who was an athlete in college. When it's gloomy out and I want to sit by the fire, Terry says, "Get your shoes on; we just have time to walk before daylight is gone." Because I know it's good for me, I comply, but in truth, I probably wouldn't have made the effort on my own. So find a compatriot who'll hold you accountable. You may break promises to yourself, but if you have a workout buddy, you'll be more likely to stay the course to fitness.

HEURISTIC

Live a healthy lifestyle so that you'll have enough energy units to spend in raising your EQ.

Take a Holiday

It helps beyond words to take yourself through the day as you would your most beloved mental patient relative, with great humor and lots of small treats.

— Anne Lamott

When I retired from the school district, I had a lot of unused sick leave because I was seldom ill. I attribute this in part to the fact that every now and then I took an R & R day—a rest and recuperation day. When I was feeling particularly tired, but not actually sick, I would call in and take a day off. It didn't happen often, but I'm convinced that I would actually have become sick had I pushed on and worked through the fatigue. By taking a strategic day off now and then, I avoided having to take two or three days or even a week or more off with a real illness. Because of my respite, I would return feeling refreshed and more energetic. I was able afterward to complete the day's work and usually most of the work from the day I missed.

The workweek has been increasing steadily for the last three decades and the culture in the workplace implies we're not pulling our weight if we don't show up everyday and put in long hours. It's seen as merely doing our job if we work on through fatigue or illness. Unfortunately we are constantly getting messages that we're supposed to be superhuman and pay no attention to not feeling up to par. TV commercials tell us we should just take a pill when we're sick and continue to carry on.

Consider instead, the attitude of the French, who view illness as an internal imbalance. When they are feeling poorly, they are more likely to take time to relax or visit a spa, or even to go on vacation, than to visit a doctor or take a pill.

Taking vacations and holidays may decrease illness and even increase your lifespan. Researchers at the State University of New York, Oswego studied middle-aged men at risk for heart disease and found that those who took frequent vacations were less likely to die from any disease, including heart problems, than those who often skipped vacations.

Cartoonist Scott Adams of *Dilbert* fame says he takes micro-vacations. "I get up and shoot pool in my office, or pet my cat, or just stare off into space. An hour doesn't go by without a micro-vacation."

HEURISTIC

Listen to your body's need for rest and take a small holiday from time to time, even when you're not sick. The renewed energy and outlook will more than make up for the time you missed, and release energy to work on raising EQ.

Rest

Don't think you will be doing less work because you sleep during the day. That's a foolish notion held by people who have no imaginations.

– Winston Churchill

What looks and feels like burnout and depression is often actually fatigue. We know how to push ourselves to meet deadlines and to complete projects, but few of us balance this with sufficient rest. A huge number of Americans are in chronic sleep debt. It is estimated that most of us sleep 20 percent less than we did 100 years ago. (Well centenarians need less sleep!) If we assume an eight hour night of sleep a century ago that means we average fewer than 6 ½ hours a night. A lot of us are getting by on even less sleep than that.

For my doctoral research, I interviewed women in significant careers who were also mothers and wives. I asked them the question, "When something's got to give to make this lifestyle work, what is it likely to be?" Almost in unison they said, "Rest." Most of these career mothers stinted themselves on relaxation and sleep to keep their lifestyles afloat. A recent survey by the National Sleep Foundation (NSF) found that 51% of those they interviewed admitted sleepiness on the job interfered with the amount and quality of their work production.

What's the answer? Sometimes we need to learn something new in order to solve a problem. But every now and then the answer lies in remembering something we learned long ago—in this case, preschool. We need to learn the art of napping. Thomas Edison got by on few hours of sleep at night, but he frequently zoned out for catnaps during the day. Other famous nappers were John F. Kennedy, Winston Churchill and Ronald Reagan. These people instinctively discovered the healing response of listening to the body's *ultradian rhythms*. In his book, *The 20 Minute Break,* Dr. Ernest Rossi explains that throughout each day, we experience natural peaks and valleys of energy.

Researchers have discovered there is a predictable pattern of these ups and downs that seem to occur in a cycle of 90 to 120 minutes. On the upswing of this cycle we experience heightened energy and mental and physical alertness. During this phase our memory and skills are at a peak and our learning ability is sharp. This is followed by a 15 to 20 minute period of low performance. If we're paying attention, we realize we need to take a break. During this downswing period, the body and mind heal and recharge for activities to come.

When we ignore this rhythm and push on through, we interrupt the natural processes of the body and set ourselves up for stress, fatigue and the ills related to these such as all manner of physical problems and psychological feelings of depression and low self-esteem. The accumulation of stress hormones in the body sets up an assault on the immune system and renders us vulnerable to whatever bug is lurking nigh.

Our instinctual response to this swing in our energies has us taking breaks when we're tired, but instead of rest and restoration, we drink stimulants like coffee, tea and caffeinated soft drinks and eat sugary, high-fat snacks, all of which set us up for a rebound effect, which has us even more fatigued during the next break.

Taking a 20-minute nap may be the ideal solution. When you nap for 20 minutes or less, you feel refreshed afterward because you haven't been down long enough to engage in REM (rapid eye-movement) sleep. Researchers at the Center for Sleep Studies at Duke University note that the average person napping takes from six to eight minutes to actually doze off. In a 20-minute nap period, that means you'll get about 12 to 14 minutes of restful sleep and arise ready to go into the upward swing of your ultradian rhythm.

Winston Churchill, who daily put on pajamas after lunch and napped, insisted that it improved his productivity. "You get two days in one—well, at least one-and-a-half," said Sir Winston.

HEURISTIC

Honor your body's need for breaks and rest by taking 15 to 20 minute breaks every 90 to 120 minutes throughout the day.

Be an Optimist

---

*Why do I tend to be optimistic? Because
the alternative is just crushing to my soul.*

– Martin Short

Lucky are those born with an inherently cheerful, upbeat disposition. My stepson, Joe, is one of these. Though he certainly has his periods of sadness and unhappiness, his default disposition is one of cheerful optimism. Optimists just have better lives, no matter what their life circumstances. According to studies they do better in school, are healthier, are more financially successful, are married longer and happier, and possibly live longer.

However, even those born with a pessimistic disposition can choose to develop an optimistic outlook. Alan Loy McGinnis read nearly 1,000 biographies for his book, *The Power of Optimism,* and found that many of the optimists had discovered techniques for overcoming feelings of depression and keeping an enthusiastic outlook.

Psychoneuroimmunologist (say that three times, fast), Paul Pearsall is of the opinion that we become pessimistic when we rely too much on our brain and in doing so become out of touch with our deeper sources of wisdom. He believes the brain is hard-wired for pessimism, which evolved as a sort of self-defense. Our early ancestors had to be on the alert for constant threats from a dangerous environment. Pearsall says we must learn to rely on "heart thinking," which brings us messages of connectedness and opens us up to the possibility that delight in some form is in store for us. What Pearsall calls heart thinking is what we have identified as the human brain, which is operative when we are using emotional intelligence.

Being optimistic makes us feel better physically. Optimists live healthier lives because their immune systems do a better job of protecting them, say researchers from the University of Kentucky at Lexington. The researchers analyzed optimistic and pessimistic law students. They found that once the pressure of law school was on, the optimists' immune systems got stronger, protecting them from colds and infections. Pessimists, however, were prone to sickness during stressful times. The study described in the *Journal of Personality and Social Psychology* states that by changing negative thought patterns, pessimists can strengthen their immune systems.

One of the ways I have discovered to help me develop a more optimistic outlook is to give myself homework assignments (another term for heuristics). This is how I do it. I have an elderly friend whose negative outlook seems to have settled around her shoulders, and it is now who she is. After an afternoon in her company I come away feeling drained of energy. Chronically miserable people are energy vampires. They are in a negative energy state and when they are in the company of higher energy types, they siphon it off. Because of this, I try to only spend time with this person when I'm feeling particularly good. Otherwise I'll come away in such a low energy state that my immune system can be compromised, and I could get sick.

After a few hours spent listening to her complain about how generally rotten people are and how nothing works the way it's supposed to, I come away from a visit vowing to catch myself whenever I fall into the whining trough. My assignment is the minute I become aware that I'm being negative, I must say two positive things for every negative one. Thus if I hear myself saying, "Oh rats, raining again," (I get a lot of opportunities to say that here in Seattle) I must say something like, " Well, it sure is good for the crops, and now I have a chance to break out my new designer umbrella."

When you sense yourself taking a pessimist outlook, think of these words by Dan Millman, author of *No Ordinary Moments,* "When you might reasonably feel upset, remember to feel unreasonably happy instead—just for the fun of it."

HEURISTIC

Do everyone a favor. Do whatever it takes to develop an optimistic outlook. It will increase the efficiency of your immune system, improve your life and raise your EQ. It will also make you easier to tolerate for the folks around you.

DEVELOPING SPIRITUAL EQ

Eventually there comes a time when most of us feel a need to make a connection to something beyond ourselves and those in our immediate surroundings. Exploration of our spiritual side is an important part of EQ development.

Suspend Disbelief

Whether or not the world is magic,
it is better to live as if it were.

— Caroline Casey

Vala had an extremely difficult childhood. She was the oldest daughter of a poor farmer in the Midwest whose family endured harsh privations during the depression. At a young age she married a man who descended into psychosis and later died. Her only child went to live with her in-laws, and then she married an unhappy man who was bitter and demanding. Though she certainly had times of unhappiness, Vala always seemed cheerful, friendly and somehow emotionally centered. I once asked her how she managed to cope with so many hardships and still be so pleasant. She responded simply, "My faith."

There are advantages to being a believer. For example, a study at the University of Santa Clara in California found that those with a religious faith or a belief in spirituality seem to benefit from an optimistic outlook, greater perceived social support and lower levels of anxiety.

But what about those of us who find that we cannot be believers in quite such an unquestioning way? Our feelings may range from skepticism to envy of the true believers. Where do you fall on the belief continuum? Do you feel okay with your belief system? If your beliefs are not supporting you, it may be time to entertain new possibilities.

What can you do if you are not a believer? You can't will yourself to believe what you don't deep in your heart believe to be true. The answer may be in trying on a heuristic called suspending disbelief. We can operate in our lives *as if* we believed something to be true. We can become what astrologer Caroline Casey calls a 'pragmatic philosopher.' That is, one who is willing to check out anything as long as it is useful. Professor of neurology Antonio Damasio calls this the "as if loop," which has to do with changes in our feelings that occur when we consciously imagine something to be true. We can actually change the way we feel about something by conjuring a particular mental image. For example, if we believed that we would be reunited with loved ones in an afterlife, we would be better able to live with their untimely deaths. If we believed that the difficult people in our lives were simply here on contract to teach us valuable life lessons, we'd find it easier to tolerate and even forgive them.

We suspend disbelief when we watch a movie or TV show or read a novel. We know these are just images on a screen or words on a page, yet they can move us to tears or laughter. We contract with ourselves to put our disbelief on the shelf for the time being and enter into another state where we operate as if we believe. Since we've all had this experience, we shouldn't find it too hard to do the same thing about spiritual practices. Wouldn't it be nice to believe that you have spiritual guides and helpers, guardian angels with you at all times to protect and serve you? Why not just assume they're there? Don't you feel safer already?

The world is our school for spiritual discovery.
— Paul Brunton

HEURISTIC

Find a spiritual practice that appeals to you and operate as if you believed the practices observed by the true believers to be the authentic path.

Respect Everything

You must learn to respect anything in which human care, effort, and affection has been invested.

– Fay Weldon

"Respect everything," breathes my yoga teacher. And because it bears repeating he says it again more softly, but with greater emphasis, "Respect *everything!*" He models this as he speaks by carefully folding the sweatshirt he has just taken off, instead of throwing it in a heap in the corner as some of us have done with our own discarded clothing as we warm up in class.

What would your life be like if you practiced this heuristic—if you showed respect for absolutely everything? Perhaps you'd begin to bring your own cup for your latté and save the landfills from another paper cup. Maybe you'd think about walking to the convenience store for milk instead of driving the car the short distance, thus saving your car engine the wear and tear of another startup and the atmosphere from the emission pollution, not to mention respecting your body and getting a little extra exercise. Cars in this country go to the scrap heap at an average age of eleven years. If we took better care of our cars, we might extend their lives by several years. Carlotta, my Volvo, is now seventeen. I figure in human years this makes her 85-years-old. She's still going strong, and I expect to drive her at least another five years—maybe ten!

If you respected everything, you might wipe the sink after washing your hands and prevent having to use abrasive chemicals to clean it after it's impossibly dirty. You would, in fact leave everyplace you'd been better than you found it.

Extending the idea of respect to the animal world, you'd get your cat or dog spayed or neutered—assuming you're not a professional breeder—thus saving the humane society from having to euthanize a litter of kittens or another stray dog.

Respecting everything would include looking after and caring for your possessions—practicing stewardship. My father, who grew up during the depression, always carefully shined his shoes and had them re-soled and re-heeled to make them last. Actually he paid my sister and me a half cent each time to polish his shoes. It was his joke. We couldn't collect the half cent so he would say he'd put it on the bill. He must've owed us at least $100 apiece by the time we grew up and left home. His shoes lasted a long time, but they always looked new because they were so well looked after.

Show respect to the people in your life. Treat all other human beings as having worth, dignity and rights equal to your own. Soul singer Aretha Franklin got it right, R-E-S-P-E-C-T is what it takes to make a relationship of any kind workable and enjoyable.

Finally, we must show respect to ourselves. Treat your own life and person as having value. Blues maestro B.B. King tells us in his song to "Respect yourself." Too often we view ourselves as expendable merchandise. Don't wind up like the old comedian who said, "If I'd known I was gonna live this long, I would've taken better care of myself." In addition, we must respect our own dreams, aspirations, goals and values as worthwhile.

HEURISTIC

Respect for everything encompasses the whole complex web of life, including ourselves, other people, animals, our possessions and the entire fragile ecosystem on which all life depends. Discover what you'd do differently if you *respect absolutely everything.*

Surrender

The world is ruled by letting things take their course. It cannot be ruled by interfering.

– Lao Tzu

Allow yourself the dignity and wisdom of saying, when appropriate, "I surrender. I can't control this; I can't fix this. I'm going to allow it to turn out however it's going to." We are all such control freaks. We go to seminars and read self-help books like this one with the illusion that we can make life turn out the way we want it to. The way it's supposed to. This is another of those things that make us crazy and cranky. We've always got all those muscles tensed, giving it body English after the ball's in the air, thinking we can get it to go through the hoop if we just hold our mouths right.

We operate too much of the time under the mistaken assumption that we can control the outcome, but the fact is that outcomes are the result of a confluence of events, some in our control and some not. By staying attached to a particular result we make ourselves crazy when it doesn't work out that way in spite of our efforts. Or we over-congratulate ourselves if it turns out the way we planned, thus setting ourselves up for disappointment if we're not so lucky the next time out.

Try this experiment. Sit for a moment and observe your breath without controlling it. Try it now. It's trickier than you'd think, isn't it? The very act of attending to it tends to change it. Keep observing it till that's all that's happening—only observing what is naturally occurring without control. What have you learned about your compulsive need to control the universe?

This is what I think we're supposed to do instead. We're supposed to make the plan, lay the groundwork, make the effort, do the work, and follow through. And then we're supposed to let go and get curious about the outcome. Michael Ray and Rochelle Myers outline a four-step process for surrender in their book *Creativity in Business:*

1. *Drop mental striving.* Wouldn't it be wonderful to think we could get where we want to go without all the struggle and strife? But a lot of us find struggling hard to give up. It feels as though it's the driving force that gets us through the day, and it may well be. The point of giving up striving is that we will get through the day anyway without striving and we won't be so exhausted at the end of it.

A few years ago when baseball great, Mark McGuire was in a slump, his coach said he was trying too hard. "What you need to do is try *easier,*" said the coach. Next time you're in the middle of a task or you're fretting about meeting a deadline and you realize your shoulders are high, your breathing is shallow and you're feeling tense and anxious, just stop and remember to try easier. Take a few deep breaths, stretch a bit and consciously let go of the struggle. Concentrate instead on the next step:

2. *Apply yourself to a task.* Surrendering doesn't mean giving up the work. Indeed, when you loosen up all those tense

muscles you'll have more available energy to actually do the work and you'll feel better while you're doing it.

So pick a task without worrying too much about its priority rating and, like the Nike ad says, "Just do it," giving no thought to the things you're *not* doing while you're doing this one. Worrying about another task while you're doing the one in front of you is like driving with your brakes on.

3. *Maintain a sense of inquiry.* Get curious. Consider it a scientific experiment. When I worked with junior high kids who had social problems, I would tell them to try out different ways to act or react to other students, with the idea of just being curious about the outcome. For example, a shy student might try saying hello to five different people a day and just observe the outcome. If she liked how it turned out, she could do more of it. If it didn't have the desired effect, she'd just try something else.

4. *Acknowledge that you don't know how it's going to turn out.* This is the part we don't like. We want to be able to predict the outcome, but the fact is, we don't really know how it's going to turn out, so we may as well give in to it and just become curious. When we allow that to happen, we are open to all sorts of serendipitous happenings, some of which may not be so wonderful but many of which will surprise and delight us if we allow it.

> *When you have got an elephant by the hind legs and he is trying to run away, it is best to let him run.*
>
> – Abraham Lincoln

HEURISTIC

Give up trying to control everything in your world and instead:
1. Drop mental striving
2. Apply yourself to a task
3. Maintain a sense of inquiry
4. Acknowledge that you don't know how it's going to turn out.

Practice Forgiveness

> *Not forgiving is like drinking rat poison*
> *and waiting for the rat to die.*
>
> — Anne Lamott

In her book, *Traveling Mercies,* Anne Lamott has a wonderful chapter on forgiveness. I'd love to copy it here, change a few of the words around and claim it as my own, the way we did when we wrote a report on Ethiopia in school, and mostly copied it out of the Encyclopaedia Britannica, thinking our teachers would never catch on. Unfortunately you'd catch on that I suddenly got to be a whole lot better writer for this one chapter. What Lamott says, basically, is that it's ourselves we're mad at when we don't forgive, and we're projecting all that venom onto someone else. But I advise you to read her hilarious and insightful book to get it in her own words. Until you get to her book, this is a difficult heuristic, but one that contributes a huge amount to raising EQ.

Like a lot of us, learning to forgive has been one of my important life lessons. Fortunately, I've got a pacer who knows the rules about this. My husband Terry is a great forgiver, maybe because he gets so much practice at having to forgive me! His theory about forgiveness is that all of us should raise our Jerk Tolerance Index (JTI). Here are the rules:

1. Everybody's a jerk from time-to-time.
2. When you've been a jerk, you must admit it afterward and apologize.
3. The other person has to forgive you after you've been one. You must also forgive yourself.
4. No one gets a monopoly on being a jerk; it's an equal opportunity experience.
5. No one gets to abuse the privilege by being one too often.

Remember how it was the last time you were being a jerk? Maybe you were in the middle of a quarrel and found yourself locked into a position you were secretly beginning to question in your own mind, but you were too invested in it by the time you realized it to admit it. And besides you were so crazy and out of control you couldn't bear to imagine the knowing, superior, slight smile that would come over your opponent's face if you admitted it. So you kept on, knowing all the while you were being childish and unreasonable—in other words, a jerk.

Now (this one's easier) imagine your partner, spouse, parent, sibling, boss, or coworker doing the same thing. No one should ever behave this way. It's really low EQ. And yet, we've all been there in both positions—the jerk and the one being jerked. Keeping yourself wrapped up in the unfairness, injuries and indignities may feel comforting. "If I forgive her it will be like saying it's okay that she did those terrible things to me. It feels disloyal to myself," protested my client, Margo. Actually, it's disloyal to yourself *not* to forgive. Carrying it around is an energy drain on you and has no effect on the unforgiven. The rat doesn't die as a result of your having drunk the rat poison, but you could get mighty sick.

Here are some ways to help you with forgiveness. Keep this in mind; make it a mantra that you repeat and repeat until you believe it: *Everyone does the best they can by the light they have to see by.*

Okay, I know. Sometimes it seems as though they have about a 10-watt bulb, but it's true they were doing their best. Most of the time when we're being a jerk, we're trying to manage our own anxiety and we lose sight of how our behavior is affecting the other party.

This ritual adapted from Feng Shui may help you to forgive those who have transgressed against you. Take out a sheet of paper and write down all of your feelings about the situation and the person who caused it, including all the exquisite ways you want them to be tortured before they die their excruciatingly painful deaths while pleading vainly for mercy. Write this in ink; a pencil won't do. Illustrate with pictures if you like; use plenty of color. When you're done with your masterpiece, place this hot little number in a bowl of water and stand back to escape the steam. Now, just let the whole thing fade out and as it disperses, let go of all that acid that's eating you alive. Be done with it.

HEURISTIC

Raise your JTI. Find a way to forgive perpetrators of injuries and insults. If you can't manage that, maybe you could try to persuade them to drink the rat poison.

Volunteer

I will act as if what I do makes a difference.

– William James

Harry, a retired school superintendent, can't seem to give up on kids. For the past several years he has volunteered in an elementary school as a reading tutor. The school is in a low income, highly mobile area; the kids move frequently and many live in chaotic conditions at home. Joey, a third grader he is tutoring, has brought his reading up to grade level with Harry's assistance. However, Joey doesn't want to cut off his contact with Harry. He continues to ask his teacher if he can go to meet with his tutor, even though he no longer needs help with his reading. Recently Harry made Joey's day when he drove to the mobile home park where Joey lives to meet the family pet—a boa constrictor!

Harry is enlarging Joey's life in ways that extend far beyond his reading comprehension level. But Harry is gaining more from the contact than Joey. He says he has a real sense of making a difference at an individual level that he missed when he was not only the boss of the whole show, but was getting paid for it, to boot. He echoes the feelings many report who volunteer.

There are other benefits of volunteering as well. Many who volunteer on a regular basis consistently report improved friendships and better relationships within their families. Service helps break rigid patterns of relating and teaches new ways of give and take with other people. This is the very essence of an EQ raising activity.

Sometimes it's hard enough to get through the daily stuff in our own lives without managing to volunteer. If you are pressed for time, many volunteer organizations offer a version of "flex-time." You give time when you can, without feeling you must sign up for an every Thursday evening appointment you know you'd never be able to keep.

My own experience with volunteering includes a stint as a crisis counselor at a mental health center. Like Harry, I had a feeling of truly contributing the time I was able to convince a lonely, would-be suicide to reconnect with the family from which she had cut off relations. I'm not volunteering regularly any place right now, but my friend Linda and I plan to give out Christmas gifts for underprivileged children at the Multi-service Center one day next week. And I know who'll come away with the best gift.

He who saves one life is as if he has saved the world.
— Talmudic Verse

HEURISTIC
Find a cause you believe in and give a little more time and money than you think you can afford. You'll get back more than you give.

Leave a Legacy

Accept the pain, cherish the joys, resolve the regrets; then can come the best of benedictions—"If I had my life to live over, I'd do it all the same."

– Joan McIntosh

What if you were able to read your own obituary, listen to the eulogy at your funeral and attend your own wake like Tom Sawyer and Huck Finn. What would your obituary say? What would the speaker say about you during the eulogy? What stories would they tell at the wake? How do you want to be remembered? Even more, how do you want to spend these days so that at the end of your life you can look back and say, "If I had my life to live over, I'd do it all the same."

Developmental psychologist Erik Erikson identified the stages we must negotiate throughout the lifespan. The stage we deal with in the last years of life is *Integrity vs. Despair.* Erikson's idea is that if we have lived integrously, to use Marge's term, we won't look back in despair over the life we've led.

I invite you to work on this final heuristic. Give some thought to how you want to spend the rest of your life and the legacy you will leave. Most of us won't be able to leave behind a lot of money, and even if you could, is that what you want to be remembered for? Re-read the description of the emotionally intelligent individual that begins on page 25. It seems to me that if each of us strives in our own way to be such a person, we will leave a worthwhile legacy.

To change your life, start immediately;
do it flamboyantly. No exceptions, no excuses.

– William James

HEURISTIC

All I can say about life is, Oh God, enjoy it.

– Bob Newhart

ABOUT THE AUTHOR

J eanne Anne Craig, Ph.D. was a school psychologist for 25 years. She is a speaker, trainer and educator, delivering keynote addresses and conducting workshops in both the private and public sectors.

Dr. Craig has graduate degrees in Educational Psychology, Human and Organizational Systems and Human Development. She is listed in Who's Who in American Colleges and Universities.

Jeanne Anne and her husband Terry have four children. They live in the Seattle area with their two cats, Cleo and Ernie.

REFERENCES
AND SUGGESTED READING

Baldwin, Christina, (1991) *Life's Companion: Journal Writing as a Spiritual Quest,* Bantam Books, New York.

Breitman, Patti; Hatch, Connie & Carlson, Richard, (2001) *How to Say No Without Feeling Guilty,* Broadway Books. New York.

Butler-Biggs, Jane, (1999) *Feng Shui in 10 Simple Lessons,* Watson-Guptill, New York.

Cameron, Julia. (1992) *The Artist's Way: A Spiritual Path to Creativity.* Tarcher, New York.

Campbell, Joseph, (1968) *The Hero With a Thousand Faces,* Bollingen, New York.

Damasio, Antonio, (1994) *Descarte's Error: Emotion, Reason and the Human Brain,* Grosset/Putnam Books, New York.

Eden, Donna, (1998) *Energy Medicine,* Tarcher, New York.

Fisher, Robert & Ury, William (1984) *Getting to Yes,* Penguin, New York.

Gardner, Howard (1983 *Frames of Mind: The Theory of Multiple Intelligences,* Basic Books, New York.

Gilbert, Roberta, (1992) *Extraordinary Relationships,* Chronimed, Minneapolis, MN.

Goleman, Daniel, (1995) *Emotional Intelligence,* Bantam Books, New York

Gottman, John, (1994) *Why Marriages Succeed or Fail: And How You Can Make Yours Last.,* Simon & Schuster, New York.

Katz, Lawrence, & Manning, Rubin (2000) *Keep Your Brain Alive,* Whitman, New York.

Kegan, Robert, (1982) *The Evolving Self,* Harvard University Press, Cambridge, MA

Klauser, Henriette Anne (2000) *Write it Down, Make it Happen.* Scribner, New York.

Kroeger, Otto, & Thuesen, Janet M. (1988), *Type Talk: The 16 Personality Types that Determine how we Live, Love, and Work,* Delta, New York.

Lamott, Anne (1999) *Traveling Mercies: Some Thoughts on Faith,* Pantheon, New York.

Lamott, Anne (1994) *Bird by Bird,* Anchor Books, New York

Levinson, Daniel J. (1978) *The Seasons of a Man's Life,* Ballantine Books, New York.

Levoy, Gregg (1997) *Callings,* Harmony Books, New York.

Miedaner, Talane, (2000) *Coach Yourself to Success: 101 tips from a personal coach for reaching your goals at work and in life,* Contemporary Books, Chicago.

McGinnis, Alan L. (1990) *The Power of Optimism,* Harper & Row, San Francisco.

Miller, Sue (1999), *While I was Gone,* Knopf, New York.

Millman, Dan, (1992) *No Ordinary Moments,* H.J. Kramer, Tiburon, CA

Myss, Caroline, (1996) *Anatomy of the Spirit,* Harmony Books, New York.

Peck, M. Scott (1997) *The Road Less Traveled* Simon & Schuster, New York

Ray, Michael & Myers, Rochelle, (1986) *Creativity in Business,* Doubleday, Garden City, New York.

Ray, Michael & Rinzler, Alan (1993) *The New Paradigm in Business,* Tarcher, New York

Schnarch, David (1997) *Passionate Marriage,* Henry Holt & Co., New York.

Shulman, Alix Kates (1996) *Drinking the Rain,* Thorndike, New York.

Suzuki, Sunryui (1988) *Zen Mind, Beginner's Mind.* Weatherhill.

von Oech, Roger (1983) *A Whack on the Side of the Head : How to unlock your mind for innovation,* Warner Books, New York.

Waller, Robert James (1999) *The Bridges of Madison County,* Thorndike, New York.

Weldon, Fay, (1984) *Letters to Alice on first reading Jane Austen,* Caroll & Graf, New York.

Winnicott, D.W. (1965) *The Maturational Process and the Facilitating Environment.* International Universities Press. New York.

INDEX

195

E

F

G

H

I

J

K

ORDER FORM

❑ Please send _____ copies of *It's Not How SMART You Are It's HOW You Are Smart* at $14.95 each, plus $3.50 shipping and handling for the first book and $1.00 for each additional book. WA residents add $1.32 per book sales tax.

❑ Please send _____ MIO heart monitor watches at $129.99 each, plus $8.00 shipping and handling for each watch. WA residents add $11.44 per watch sales tax.

(Canadian orders must be accompanied by a postal money order in U.S. funds.)

To Order:
- By phone: (425) 822-8159   Toll free (866) 822-8159
- By fax: (425) 803-0143
- By e-mail: TheRightSmarts@aol.com
- By mail: Craine Press
            218 Main Street, #339B
            Kirkland, WA 98033

Method of Payment:
My check or money order for $ _____ is enclosed.

Or please charge my ❑ Visa ❑ MasterCard ❑ Discover ❑ American Express

NAME _____

ORGANIZATION _____

ADDRESS _____

CITY/STATE/ZIP _____

PHONE _____

CARD # _____ EXP DATE _____

SIGNATURE _____

■ ■

Children of the Dump (as described on page 147). For information regarding this charitable program or to send a donation, write to:

Children of the Dump
718 Griffin Ave PMB #207
Enumclaw, WA 98022-3462